KWELLER PREP

COMMON CORE

GRADE 4

ENGLISH LANGUAGE ARTS

Kweller Prep

Developed by a lawyer, Kweller Prep is an established supplemental education service with a 15-year track record of success in preparing students for specialized middle-school, high-school, college entrance, and graduate school exams. With thousands of acceptances to date, Kweller Prep has built a time-tested learning program with unsurpassed performance. Our competitive advantage is the way in which we operate; we focus on each child individually to ensure success.

Our rigorous program is designed for ambitious students to help them achieve their academic goals. Tutoring centers in Queens and Manhattan serve as learning incubators where parents, students, teachers, tutors, and counselors alike can learn from one another and grow. Nearly every tutor at Kweller Prep is the first one in his or her family to attend a Specialized High School or Top University on a scholarship.

Kweller Prep was created by the vision of Frances Kweller, attorney at law. She was the first one in her immediate family to attend both a top university (New York University - Steinhardt School of Education) and Graduate Program (Juris Doctorate - Hofstra University School of Law). In short, Kweller Prep is designed to help get you where you want to go! 2 locations! Forest Hills, Queens and midtown Manhattan.

Email : info@kwellerprep.com

Website: **www.KwellerPrep.com**

First Edition January 2019.

This is the first edition so if you find any errors, please correct the error and then take a picture of the correction and the page number. Please email it to info@kwellerprep.com. Ms. Kweller will you $1 for any typo you find before May 1, 2019.

Copyright © 2019 by Origins Publications

Written by: Kweller Prep in collaboration with Origins Publications

All rights reserved. This book or any portion thereof may not be reproduced or used in any manner whatsoever without the express written permission of the publisher.

ISBN: 13: 978-1-948255-73-8

The NY State Department of Education is not affiliated with Kweller Prep or Origins Publications and has not endorsed the contents of this book.

Origins Publications
New York, NY, USA
Email:info@originspublications.com

TABLE OF CONTENTS

Introduction 4
How To Use This Book 5
Test Prep Tips 6

Reading: Literature 7
Understand Text: Refer to Details and Draw Inferences (RL.4.1) 8
Determine Theme & Summarize Text (RL.4.2) 12
Describe Character, Setting and Events (RL.4.3) 16
Determine Word Meaning in Text (RL.4.4) 20
Explain Structural Differences between Poems, Drama and Prose(RL.4.5)...... 23
Compare and Contrast Point of View (RL.4.6) 26
Using Images to Understand Text (RL.4.7) 30
Compare & Contrast Themes/Events in Different Cultural Stories/Myths (RL.4.9).......... 37

Reading: Information 42
Understand Text: Refer to Details and Draw Inferences (RI.4.1)........................ 43
Determine Main Idea & Summarize Text (RI.4.2) 47
Use Details to Explain Events, Procedures & Ideas in Text (RI.4.3) 51
Determine Word Meaning in Text (RI.4.4) 55
Describe Structure of Events, Ideas or Information in Text (RI.4.5) 59
Compare & Contrast Firsthand & Secondhand Accounts (RI.4.6) 63
Use Images/Diagrams to Understand Text (RI.4.7).. 67
Explain How Authors Use Evidence to Support Point of View (RI.4.8) 71
Integrate Information from Two Texts (RI.4.9).. 74

Language 79
Have Command of Grammar & Usage (L.4.1.A - L.4.1.G) 80
Know Capitalization, Punctuation & Spelling (L.4.2.A - L.4.2.D)........................ 86
Use Appropriate Language Conventions To Convey Ideas (L.4.3.A - L.4.3.C) .. 90
Determine Meaning of Unknown Words When Reading (L.4.4.A - L.4.4.C) 94
Understand Figurative Language (L.4.5.A - L.4.5.C) 100
Know & Use General Academic/Domain-Specific Words (L.4.6)..................... 104

Answer Key and Explanations 107

Practice Tests... 125
Practice Test One.. 127
Practice Test One Answer Key & Explanations 153
Practice Test Two.. 157
Practice Test Two Answer Key & Explanations 183

INTRODUCTION

Common Core Standards

States all across the USA have implemented rigorous standards called the "Common Core Standards."

These standards, or learning goals, outline what students in each grade should learn each year. They emphasize just how important the new goals are: they can help show whether students are on the right track to college and beyond, even when the students are years from those life stages.

State English Language Arts (ELA) Assessments

State ELA assessments are designed to determine whether students have mastered grade level appropriate reading, writing and language skills.

The ELA assessment is usually given annually in grades 3-8, and is administered in either computer-based or paper-based format.

Question Format on State ELA Assessments

All questions will be based on close reading of informational and literary texts, including paired texts. There are three major question formats on State ELA exams.

Multiple-Choice Questions: For multiple-choice questions, students select the correct response from four answer choices. These questions ask students to analyze different aspects of a given text, including central idea, style elements, character and plot development, and vocabulary. Reading and Language Standards will be assessed using multiple-choice questions.

Short-Response Questions: These are single questions which ask the student to make an inference (a claim, position, or conclusion) based on his or her analysis of the passage, and then provide two pieces of text-based evidence to support his or her answer. In responding to these questions, students are expected to write in complete sentences. Responses require no more than three complete sentences. Short-response questions will primarily assess reading, but will also require writing and command of language.

Extended-Response Questions: Extended-response questions are essay questions designed to measure a student's ability to write from sources, and prompt students to communicate a clear and coherent analysis of one or two texts.

HOW TO USE THIS BOOK

The objective of this book is to provide students, educators, and parents with materials that help students improve their mastery and understanding of the Common Core Standards and to help students succeed on aligned State ELA assessments.

Students can practice key material by doing the standard-tethered skill-building exercises. Students can also take practice tests based on official tests so they review what they have learned and can become accustomed to how content is presented in State assessments.

This Book Includes:

- 228 skill-building exercises organised by standard in order to help students learn and review concepts in the order that they will likely be presented in the classroom. These worksheets also help identify weaknesses, and highlight and strengthen the skills needed to excel on the actual exam. A variety of question types are included in the worksheets to help students build skills in answering questions in multiple formats, and to help students stay engaged while they work through problems.

- Practice test materials that are based on the official assessments released by State test administrator, and include similar question types and the same rigorous content found on the official assessments. By using these materials, students will become familiar with the types of items they may see on the real test. Two practice tests are included in this book.

- Answer keys with detailed explanations to help students not make the same mistakes again. These explanations help clear up common misconceptions and indicate how students might arrive at an answer to a question.

- Answer keys also identify the standard/s that the question is assessing. If a student is having difficulty in one area, encourage the student to improve in that area by practicing the specific set of skills in the workbook.

- Test prep tips to help students approach the test strategically and with confidence.

TEST PREP TIPS

First of all, remind your student to pay attention in class throughout the year, asking questions as needed on homework and classwork. The Language Arts curriculum should follow the exact standards and skills that will be tested on the end-of-year assessment.

One of the best ways to prepare for a reading test is by—of course—reading. In the months leading up to the test, students should read a certain amount of pages or minutes weekly from a book that they enjoy. Reading consistently will improve a student's reading comprehension and enhance her vocabulary, two skills that are crucial to success on the exam.

Another extremely effective strategy is to practice, practice, practice. Have your student work on practice questions and complete several full length practice tests. Our practice tests are a great place to start.

However, simply answering the questions and then moving on will not yield much improvement. If a student misses a question, discuss why the correct answer is indeed correct. Come up with alternate approaches to this question type that may work better in the future. Have your student explain his answer to each question. This gives you the opportunity to reinforce logical thinking and correct misconceptions as needed. Plus, it's good practice for finding evidence to support a claim, perhaps the key skill on ELA reading assessments.

Prior to the test, students should have a solid night of sleep and eat a nourishing breakfast.

Avoiding excessive test anxiety is important, so be sure to avoid over-emphasizing the test or inadvertently causing your student to feel too much stress or pressure.

In addition, teach your student general test-taking strategies such as the following:

Narrow down your answer choices by using process of elimination. This involves crossing out obviously wrong answers to increase your chances of finding the correct answer.

If you get stuck on a question, skip it and come back to it after answering easier questions.

Remember that no one is expected to answer every single correction correctly. Don't panic when you get stuck on a question. Take a deep breath and remember that you are intelligent and prepared.

If you follow the advice here, your student should be well on her way to a stress-free and successful performance on this important assessment.

READING: LITERATURE

UNDERSTAND TEXT

RL.4.1: Refer to details and examples in a text when explaining what the text says explicitly and when drawing inferences from the text.

Directions: Read the passage and answer the questions below.

Passage 1: Adapted selection from *The Dragon Tamers* (Part 1)
by Edith Nesbit

1   There was once an old, old castle—it was so old that its walls, towers, and arches had crumbled to ruins, and of all its old splendor there were only two little rooms left. It was here that John the farrier had set up his forge. John used the forge to heat and shape metal horseshoes for horses. No one asked any rent for the rooms in the ruin, because, in fact, the castle was abandoned.

2   One day, through the hammering a noise came louder and louder, and the more John and his wife tried not to hear it, the more they had to. It was like the noise of some great creature purring, purring, purring. It came from the great dungeon down below with the broken steps that went down into the dark and ended no one knew where.

3   Eventually, John went to the winding stairs and held up the lantern. Half of it was empty, but the other side was not. It was quite full, and what it was full of was Dragon.

4   The dragon caught John by the leg. As it moved it rattled like a great bunch of keys. As it moved, the castle also heaved with the dragon's mighty movement.

5   "Oh, I'm glad you finally found me, as I should like you to do a job for me," said the dragon. "One of my wings has got some of the screws out of it just above the joint. You mend my wing, and then I'll go out and eat up all the townsfolk, and if you do a really smart job of it, I'll eat you last."

1. What is the greatest danger to John and his family in this story?
    A. The castle is abandoned.
    B. There is no light in the stairwell.
    C. A dragon is living in the castle with John and his family.
    D. John is not paying rent for the two rooms in the castle.

2. Which statement best explains why John does not need to pay money (rent) to live in the castle?
    A. John likes living with the dragon.
    B. The two rooms that the family lives in are cramped.
    C. John offers an important service to the community by making shoes for the town's horses.
    D. No-one collects money for the castle's rent.

READING: LITERATURE

3. Re-read this sentence from the text: "There was once an old, old castle—it was so old that its walls, towers, and arches had crumbled to ruins, and of all its old splendor there were only two little rooms left."
   What do you think the word splendor means in the above passage?
   - **A.** antiques
   - **B.** magnificence
   - **C.** sweetness
   - **D.** architecture

4. The following question has two parts. First, answer Part A. Then, answer Part B.

Part A
What is the most convincing reason that the dragon wants to be found?
- **A.** The dragon wants someone to help it fix its wing.
- **B.** The dragon is concerned that the castle is falling down.
- **C.** The dragon wants to play tag with John.
- **D.** The dragon wants John to be scared and leave the castle.

Part B
What evidence from the text best supports your answer in A?
- **A.** "The dragon caught John by the leg." (Paragraph 4).
- **B.** "As it moved it rattled like a great bunch of keys." (Paragraph 4).
- **C.** "...it was so old that its walls, towers, and arches had crumbled to ruins..." (Paragraph 1).
- **D.** "I should like you to do a job for me," said the dragon. "One of my wings has got some of the screws out of it just above the joint." (Paragraph 5).

Directions: Read the poem and answer the questions below.

St. Patrick's Day
by Jean Blewett

There's an Isle, a green Isle, set in the sea,
  Here's to the Saint that blessed it!
And here's to the billows wild and free
  That for centuries have caressed it!

Here's to the day when the men that roam
  Send longing eyes o'er the water!
Here's to the land that still spells home
  To each loyal son and daughter!

Here's to old Ireland—fair, I ween,
  With the blue skies stretched above her!
Here's to her shamrock warm and green,
  And here's to the hearts that love her!

5. Based on the poem, you can infer that the country is...
   - **A.** attached to other countries
   - **B.** an island
   - **C.** landlocked
   - **D.** very cold

6. How does the poet feel about the country?
   - **A.** The poet feels glad to be away from the country.
   - **B.** The poet once had a lot of fun in the country.
   - **C.** The poet loves and cherishes the country.
   - **D.** The poet wishes there was more to do in the country.

7. What does the word "fair" mostly likely mean in the first line of the final stanza?
   - **A.** beautiful
   - **B.** okay
   - **C.** equal
   - **D.** odd

8. What country is the poem about?
   - **A.** England
   - **B.** Ireland
   - **C.** Russia
   - **D.** Greenland

Directions: Read the short passage and answer the question below.

Dogs used to dig holes and bury their bones to keep them safe from other dogs and animals. Even though most dogs have enough food to eat today, they still want to bury their favorite bones and toys because of their natural instincts.

9. Based on the passage above, make an inference about why dogs today still hide their bones and toys.
    - **A.** They like to save it as a snack for later.
    - **B.** They want to hide them from other dogs.
    - **C.** They think it is a fun game to play with their owners.
    - **D.** They enjoy digging holes and finding bones.

Directions: Read the short passage and answer the question below.

Jerome was about halfway through his math homework when he glanced at his watch. "Oh no!" he said aloud. He threw on his soccer jersey and quickly put on his favorite cleats. He grabbed his soccer bag and sprinted out the door. "Nice of you to join us, Jerome!" his soccer coach bellowed as Jerome made his way onto the field.

10. What can you infer based on the evidence in the paragraph?
    - **A.** Jerome is late to soccer practice.
    - **B.** Jerome really loves soccer.
    - **C.** Jerome slept late and missed soccer.
    - **D.** Jerome isn't very organized.

Directions: Read the short passage and answer the question below.

Jasmine saw her friend Allison walking slowly into the classroom. Allison was late again, and she looked upset. She has to walk her younger siblings to daycare each morning on her way to school. The daycare is ¼ of a mile away from her school, and she is usually late to class. Allison needs to wake up early in the morning to walk her siblings to daycare and doesn't get enough sleep at night, which puts her in a bad mood and she is often forgetful. Yesterday she forgot her homework and today she forgot a pencil. Jasmine doesn't want her friend, Allison, to have a bad day at school, so she opens up her pencil case to provide an extra pencil for Allison.

11. Make an inference about why Jasmine is looking for an extra pencil. Explain your answer using evidence from the text.

READING: LITERATURE

DETERMINE THEME & SUMMARIZE TEXT

RL.4.2 Determine a theme of a story, drama, or poem from details in the text; summarize the text.

Directions: Read the poem and answer the questions that follow.

Passage 1: Two Little Kittens
by: Anonymous

Two little kittens, one stormy night,
Began to quarrel, and then to fight;
One had a mouse, the other had none,
And that's the way the quarrel begun.

"I'll have that mouse," said the biggest cat;
"You'll have that mouse? We'll see about that!"
"I will have that mouse," said the tortoise-shell;
And, spitting and scratching, on her sister she fell.

I told you before 'twas a stormy night
When these two little kittens began to fight;
The old woman seized her sweeping broom,
And swept the two kittens right out of the room.

The ground was covered with frost and snow,
And the two little kittens had nowhere to go;
So, they laid them down on the mat at the door,
While the old woman finished sweeping the floor.

Then they crept in, as quiet as mice,
All wet with the snow, and cold as ice,
For they found it was better, that stormy night,
To lie down and sleep than to quarrel and fight.

1. Why are the kittens fighting?
    A. One cat likes storms and the other doesn't.
    B. One cat has a mouse and the other doesn't.
    C. One cat has a bigger mouse than the other.
    D. One cat wants to eat and one wants to play.

2. There are two parts for this question. First, answer Part A, then Part B.

Part A.
What is the main moral of this poem?
   A. It's better to get along than to fight.
   B. Don't go outside on a stormy day.
   C. It's better to play inside than outside.
   D. Kittens should always be quieter than mice.

Part B.
Which piece of evidence from the poem supports your answer from question 2?
   A. "The old woman seized her sweeping broom,
      And swept the two kittens right out of the room."
   B. "I told you before 'twas a stormy night
      When these two little kittens began to fight;"
   C. "Then they crept in, as quiet as mice,
      All wet with the snow, and cold as ice…"
   D. "For they found it was better, that stormy night,
      To lie down and sleep than to quarrel and fight."

3. In lines 11 and 12, why did the old woman sweep "the two kittens right out of the room?"

_____
_____
_____

4. Summarize this poem. Include details about how the setting contributes to the overall theme of the poem. Support your conclusions with evidence from the text.

_____
_____
_____
_____
_____

Directions: Read the passage and answer the questions below.

Passage 2: I survived

1   In 1971, I was seventeen years old and flying to the Peruvian rainforest to visit my father, a scientist studying plants, animals and their habitats. About thirty minutes into the flight, lightning began striking around the plane, and passengers started screaming.

2   Next, lightning hit the plane, and the airplane ripped in half. I was somehow ejected from the plane, still buckled into my seat. I woke up the next morning with some cuts and a broken collarbone. I was so surprised that I was still alive! Then, I realized how alone I was in the jungle.

3   I didn't have any food with me, but I found a bag of candy that someone must have brought on the plane. I remembered that my father had told me to follow water if I was ever lost in the jungle. I found a stream and started walking beside it.

4   Soon, I ran out of candy. My father also taught me that a lot of the food in the jungle was poisonous, so I just drank lots of water from the stream. By the tenth day, I could barely walk. I knew that I desperately needed food. Eventually, I saw a small hut. I went into the hut and fell asleep.

5   In the morning, the sounds of men's voices woke me. I explained to the men what had happened to me. They gave me food, and I was reunited with my father a day later. Of the 92 passengers on my flight, only I survived.

5. Why is it important to mention that the author is going to visit her father, a scientist studying plants, animals and their habitats?
    A. The author wants to let the reader know that her father's knowledge of the jungle helps save her.
    B. The author wants the reader to know that her father shouldn't have let her fly alone.
    C. It gives the reader interesting background information about the author.
    D. The author wants us to understand that she had a close relationship with her father.

6. Which of the following is one of the main themes of this passage?
    A. Humans can live for weeks without food.
    B. Survival skills can help you stay alive in the wild.
    C. Airplane crashes can be very frightening.
    D. Don't fly in a plane over a jungle.

READING: LITERATURE

7. Why does the author include Paragraph 4?
   A. To show that the author might not have survived if she didn't find the hut when she did.
   B. To show how eating too much candy affected the author.
   C. To explain why the author decided to give up.
   D. To show readers that the author shouldn't have gone into a stranger's hut.

8. Only the author survived the plane crash. Summarize how the author survived and stayed alive in the jungle. Include two details from the text.

DESCRIBE CHARACTER, SETTING, AND EVENTS

RL.4.3 Describe in depth a character, setting, or event in a story or drama, drawing on specific details in the text (e.g., a character's thoughts, words, or actions).

Directions: Read the passage and answer the questions below.

Passage 1: The Princess and the Pea
by Hans Christian Andersen

1   ONCE upon a time there was a prince who wanted to marry a princess; but she would have to be a real princess. He travelled all over the world to find one, but nowhere could he get what he wanted. There were princesses enough, but it was difficult to find out whether they were real ones. There was always something about them that was not as it should be. So he came home again and was sad, for he would have liked very much to have a real princess.

2   One evening a terrible storm came on; there was thunder and lightning, and the rain poured down in torrents. Suddenly a knocking was heard at the city gate, and the old queen went to open it.

3   There was a princess standing out there in front of the gate. But, good gracious! what a sight the rain and the wind had made her look. The water ran down from her hair and clothes; it ran down into the toes of her shoes and out again at the heels. And yet she said that she was a real princess.

4   Well, we'll soon find that out, thought the old queen. But she said nothing, went into the bed-room, took all the bedding off the bedstead, and laid a pea on the bottom; then she took twenty mattresses and laid them on the pea, and then twenty eider-down beds on top of the mattresses.

5   On this the princess had to lie all night. In the morning she was asked how she had slept.

6   Oh, very badly! said she. I have scarcely closed my eyes all night. Heaven only knows what was in the bed, but I was lying on something hard, so that I am black and blue all over my body. Its horrible!

7   Now they knew that she was a real princess because she had felt the pea right through the twenty mattresses and the twenty eider-down beds.

8   Nobody but a real princess could be as sensitive as that.

9   So the prince asked her to be his wife. Now, he knew that he had married a real princess; and the pea was put in the museum, where it may still be seen, if no one has stolen it.

10   There, that is a true story.

1. Why does the queen require the princess to sleep on twenty mattresses on top of a pea?
   A. She believes that the prince is being too picky about finding a wife.
   B. She wants to prove to the prince that there's no such thing as a true princess.
   C. She wants to determine if the young woman is truly a princess.
   D. She wants to prove that the princess can detect a tiny pea.

2. Which detail from the story best supports the claim that the princess was a real princess?
   A. "But, good gracious! what a sight the rain and the wind had made her look."
   B. "…she had felt the pea right through the twenty mattresses and the twenty eider-down beds."
   C. "…and the pea was put in the museum, where it may still be seen, if no one has stolen it."
   D. "And yet she said that she was a real princess."

3. Based on the events in the story, which word best describes the prince at the end of the story?
   A. satisfied
   B. sleepy
   C. concerned
   D. sad

4. How does the setting and character description in paragraphs 2 and 3 build suspense about the young woman's character? Give evidence from the text to support your answer.

READING: LITERATURE   17

Directions: Read the passage and answer the questions below.

Passage 2: The Ants & the Grasshopper
by Aesop

1   One bright day in late autumn a family of Ants were bustling about in the warm sunshine, drying out the grain they had stored up during the summer, when a starving Grasshopper, his fiddle under his arm, came up and humbly begged for a bite to eat.

2   "What!" cried the Ants in surprise, "haven't you stored anything away for the winter? What in the world were you doing all last summer?"

3   "I didn't have time to store up any food," whined the Grasshopper; "I was so busy making music that before I knew it the summer was gone."

4   The Ants shrugged their shoulders in disgust.

5   "Making music, were you?" they cried. "Very well; now dance!" And they turned their backs on the Grasshopper and went on with their work.

6   There's a time for work and a time for play.

5. Setting is the place or surroundings where a story takes place. Write a phrase that describes the setting in the column titled Phrase that Describes the Setting. Then select two pieces of supporting evidence from the text and write them in the column titled Evidence From "The Ants & the Grasshopper."

Phrase that Describes the Setting	Evidence From "The Ants & the Grasshopper"

6. Reread paragraph 1. The author uses the adjective humbly to describe how the grasshopper approaches the ants. Based on this adjective, how is the grasshopper feeling at this moment?
    A. angry and demanding
    B. meek and embarrassed
    C. happy and full
    D. sympathetic and giving

7. The following question has two parts. First answer Part A. Then, answer Part B.

Part A

What can you infer about the ants in the story?

    A. They appreciate the grasshopper's music.
    B. They are hopeful that the grasshopper will help them.
    C. They believe the grasshopper was foolish.
    D. They feel sorry for the grasshopper.

Part B

Which detail from the text supports the answer for Part A?

    A. "…a starving Grasshopper, his fiddle under his arm, came up and humbly begged for a bite to eat."
    B. "The Ants shrugged their shoulders in disgust."
    C. "One bright day in late autumn…"
    D. "…a family of Ants were bustling about in the warm sunshine…"

8. When the ants say, "Very well; now dance!" what does it reveal about their belief about the grasshopper's actions over the summer? Use information from the text in your explanation.

DETERMINE WORD MEANING IN TEXT

RL.4.4 Determine the meaning of words and phrases as they are used in a text, including those that allude to significant characters found in mythology (e.g., Herculean).

Directions: Read the passage and answer the questions below.

Passage: A Golden Moment

1   The moment was here. Jessie shook out her arms and leaned left and right, stretching. She took a deep breath, exhaling slowly to blow out the butterflies that had been fluttering in her stomach. She was trying to beat the world record for number of baskets made in one minute while riding a unicycle. She had been practicing for ages. All she needed was one more than the current record of 33.

2   The officials from the World Record Book were ready, stiffly holding their recording sheets, video recorders in hand. Jessie stared at their logs, wondering if her name would ever be in that book. She worried briefly if her Achilles heel would be her downfall—the last time she practiced a cramp in her shoulder kept her from making baskets from the left side. But before she had too much time to worry, the officials called her name. There was no turning back.

3   A particularly stern man with a stopwatch told Jessie to take her place. He towered over Jessie, unsmiling, and examined his clipboard. He frowned as he inspected the stopwatch. Jessie mounted her unicycle, ball in hand. As the man counted down, "In 5, 4, 3, 2, 1, begin!" Jessie cycled around the court, preparing for her first shot. At the official's signal she began shooting.

4   The first 30 shots came easily, but then Jessie missed. And missed again. "This is a catastrophe," she thought miserably. With just 15 seconds to go, Jessie needed to make four more shots. And then, as she'd done a hundred times before, Jessie relaxed her body. 31, 32, 33... the next few shots sailed in. Just one more to go! Shot 34 bounced around the rim, teetering on the edge before falling through the hoop.

5   "Yes!" Jessie and the crowd roared together! She hopped off her bike just in time for her best friend Sam to squeeze her neck. The officials, now smiling, walked over with a ribbon printed with "World Record Holder." The stern official from earlier shook Jessie's hand, "You certainly seem to have the Midas Touch, young lady," he congratulated her.

6   Jessie felt her heart explode with pride. She had done it!

1. What does the word mounted mean in paragraph 3?
   A. attached
   B. rode
   C. climbed on
   D. put away

2. What word or phrase could be substituted for the word catastrophe in paragraph 4?
   A. disaster
   B. lucky break
   C. exciting event
   D. dream

3. In paragraph 4, what effect does the word teetering have on the action of the story?
   A. It makes the reader doubt that Jessie has been practicing.
   B. It adds suspense, as the reader wonders if Jessie will make it.
   C. It advances the plot by telling the reader that Jessie has done this hundreds of times before.
   D. It implies that Jessie will be disappointed in the end.

4. Reread the following sentence.
   "And then, as she'd done a hundred times before, Jessie relaxed her body. 31, 32, 33… the next few shots sailed in."
   What effect does the word sailed have on the meaning of the text?

   _____

   _____

   _____

5. Reread this sentence from paragraph 1.
   "She took a deep breath, exhaling slowly to blow out the butterflies that had been fluttering in her stomach."
   In the sentence, the phrase "butterflies…fluttering in her stomach" implies that:
   A. Jessie is hungry.
   B. Jessie is nervous.
   C. Jessie needs to stretch more.
   D. Jessie's time is running out.

6. Define the meaning of the word "stern" as it is used in the passage (paragraph 3). Then distinguish two details from the text that best support your understanding of the word and explain how the evidence supports your definition.

Definition:		
	Evidence from the text	**Explanation of how text evidence supports the definition**
#1		
#2		

7. The following question has two parts. First, answer Part A. Then, answer Part B.

Part A

Based on what you know about Jessie from this passage, how might you describe an Achilles heel as the author uses it in paragraph 2?

   A. a weakness
   B. an injured foot
   C. an advantage
   D. a strong arm

Part B

Which detail from the text helps the reader understand the meaning of the phrase Achilles heel in Part A?

   A. "She worried"
   B. "her downfall"
   C. "she practiced"
   D. "her shoulder"

8. What does it mean to have the Midas Touch? How does this reference help the reader understand the task the character faced?

22   **READING: LITERATURE**

EXPLAIN STRUCTURAL DIFFERENCES BETWEEN POEMS, DRAMA AND PROSE

RL.4.5 Explain major differences between poems, drama, and prose, and refer to the structural elements of poems (e.g., verse, rhythm, meter) and drama (e.g., casts of characters, settings, descriptions, dialogue, stage directions) when writing or speaking about a text.

Directions: Read the passages and answer the questions below.

Passage 1: Adapted excerpt from "Rikki-tikki-tavi" from The Jungle Books, Volume Two.
by Rudyard Kipling

1   This is the story of the great war that Rikki-tikki-tavi fought single-handed, through the bath-rooms of the big bungalow in Segowlee dwelling. Darzee, the tailor-bird, helped him, and Chuchundra, the musk-rat, who never comes out into the middle of the floor, but always creeps round by the wall, gave him advice; but Rikki-tikki did the real fighting.

2   He was a mongoose, rather like a little cat in his fur and his tail, but quite like a weasel in his head and his habits. His eyes and the end of his restless nose were pink; he could scratch himself anywhere he pleased, with any leg, front or back, that he chose to use; he could fluff up his tail till it looked like a bottle-brush, and his war-cry, as he scuttled through the long grass, was: "Rikk-tikk-tikki-tikki-tchk!"

3   One day, a high summer flood washed him out of the burrow where he lived with his father and mother, and carried him, kicking and clucking, down a roadside ditch. He found a little wisp of grass floating there, and clung to it till he lost his senses. When he woke up, he was lying in the hot sun on the middle of a garden path, wet and dirty, and a small boy was saying: "Here's a dead mongoose. Let's have a funeral."

4   "No," said his mother; "let's take him in and dry him. Perhaps he isn't really dead."

5   They took him into the house, and a big man picked him up between his finger and thumb, and said he was not dead but half choked; so they wrapped him in cotton-wool, and warmed him, and he opened his eyes and sneezed.

6   "Now," said the big man (he was an Englishman who had just moved into the bungalow); "don't frighten him, and we'll see what he'll do."

7   It is the hardest thing in the world to frighten a mongoose, because he is so curious. The motto of all the mongoose family is "Run and find out"; and Rikki-tikki was a true mongoose. He looked at the cotton-wool, decided that it was not good to eat, ran all around the table, sat up and put his fur in order, scratched himself, and jumped on the small boy's shoulder.

Passage 2: Dust of Snow
by Robert Frost

The way a crow
Shook down on me
The dust of snow
From a hemlock tree

Has given my heart
A change of mood
And saved some part
Of a day I had rued.

Passage 3: Excerpt from The Pirates' Adventure

Characters: Pirate Pete, Patchy Parrot, Pegleg Perry, Other Pirates

Act 1

(The crew is on a pirate ship, and just finishing various maintenance tasks.)

Pirate Pete: Ahoy, mateys! It's time to once again return to the deep blue sea!

Pegleg Perry: Yes! We need to find the prince's treasure.

Patchy Parrot: Awk. Treasure?

Pegleg Perry: The prince's treasure is a legend, but only the bravest pirate crew is courageous enough to search for it.

Pirate Pete: The ship is ready, we leave at dawn!

Patchy Parrot: Awk. We leave at dawn!

All: Yo-ho-ho!

1. What is the structure of the text in Passage 1 ("Rikki Tikki Tavi").
    A. poetry
    B. drama
    C. prose.
    D. verse.

2. Passage 2 (Dust of Snow) includes all of the following structural elements EXCEPT?
    A. rhyme
    B. rhythm
    C. stanzas
    D. dialogue

3. How is Passage 1 ("Rikki Tikki Tavi") organized?
   A. paragraphs
   B. stage directions
   C. verses
   D. writing

4. What are the structural elements used in a drama and what purpose do they serve?

   _____

   _____

   _____

   _____

5. What is the function of the dialogue in Passage 1 ("Rikki Tikki Tavi")?
   A. It helps the reader understand what is happening.
   B. It gives the writing a consistent rhythm and pattern.
   C. It helps the reader understand the mongoose's point of view.
   D. It tells the reader all the background knowledge s/he needs to understand the story.

6. Re-read Passage 3 ("The Pirate's Adventure). What is the function of the stage directions in this passage?
   A. They help the reader predict the solution.
   B. They help the reader understand the setting.
   C. They help the reader know characters descriptions.
   D. They help the reader know who is speaking.

7. The following question has two parts. First answer Part A. Then, answer Part B.

Part A
   Read the following poem that introduces the story "Rikki-tikki-tavi"(Passage 1). What structural element do the poem and the actual story have in common?

   At the hole where he went in
   Red-Eye called to Wrinkle-Skin.
   Hear what little Red-Eye saith:
   "Nag, come up and dance with death!"

   Eye to eye and head to head,
   (Keep the measure, Nag.)

READING: LITERATURE 25

This shall end when one is dead;
(At thy pleasure, Nag.)

Turn for turn and twist for twist-
(Run and hide thee, Nag.)
Hah! The hooded Death has missed!
(Woe betide thee, Nag!)

    A. rhythm
    B. dialogue
    C. rhyme
    D. stage directions

Part B

    Who does much of the poem address?
        A. Rikki-tikki-tavi
        B. Nag
        C. Red-Eye
        D. Wrinkle-Skin

8. Re-read Passage 1 ("Rikki Tikki Tavi") and Passage 2 (Dust of Snow). Complete the comparison chart by analyzing the text structure to identify and explain the literary format of each passage.

"Rikki Tikki Tavi"	Structural Elements	Text Evidence	Explanation
Literary Format: _____	1. _____ 2. _____	1. _____ 2. _____	1. _____ 2. _____
"Dust of Snow"	Structural Elements	Text Evidence	Explanation
Literary Format: _____	1. _____ 2. _____	1. _____ 2. _____	1. _____ 2. _____

COMPARE AND CONTRAST POINT OF VIEW

RL.4.6 Compare/contrast the point of view from which different stories are narrated, including the difference between first- and third-person narrations.

Directions: Read the passages and answer the questions below.

Passage 1 : Excerpt from The Wonderful Wizard of Oz
by Lyman Frank Baum

1   The Scarecrow found a tree full of nuts and filled Dorothy's basket with them, so that she would not be hungry for a long time. She thought this was very kind and thoughtful of the Scarecrow, but she laughed heartily at the awkward way in which the poor creature picked up the nuts. His padded hands were so clumsy that he dropped almost as many as he put in the basket. But the Scarecrow did not mind how long it took him to fill the basket, for it enabled him to keep away from the fire, as he feared a spark might get into his straw and burn him up.

Passage 2: Adapted Excerpt of the "The Myth of Icarus and Daedelus"

1   There was once a young man named Icarus. He and his father Daedelus were imprisoned by an evil man on an island. They were surrounded by high walls, and the island was surrounded by water.

2   Daedelus was an inventor. He invented wings made from bird feathers and wax. He wanted to use the wings to escape. But because of the wax, the wings would melt if they got hot. So Daedelus warned Icarus not to fly too close to the sun. You can probably guess what happened next.

3   Daedulus and Icarus used the wings to fly away from the island. "Remember," said the father, "never fly very low or very high. The Earth's fog will weigh you down, but the blaze of the sun will melt your feathers apart if you go too near."

4   They escaped across the sea. But Icarus was too excited about flying. He didn't remember his father's instructions and enjoyed the feeling of flying. He flew too close to the hot sun. The wax melted, and he fell into the sea.

5   Daedelus only saw the feathers floating on the water, and knew that Icarus had drowned. He was filled with sadness. He named the nearest island Icaria, in memory of his beloved son. And he never flew again.

1.   From what point of view is the story told in Passage 1?
   A. first-person
   B. second-person
   C. third-person
   D. limited view

READING: LITERATURE   27

2. From what point of view is most of Passage 2 told?
    A. first-person
    B. second-person
    C. third-person
    D. limited view

3. The following question has two parts. First, answer Part A. Then, answer Part B.

Part A

In which paragraph of Passage 2 does the point of view shift to second-person for a moment?
    A. paragraph 2
    B. paragraph 3
    C. paragraph 4
    D. paragraph 5

Part B

What evidence from the text shows you the 2nd person point of view?
    A. "He named the nearest island Icaria, in memory of his beloved son. "
    B. "They escaped across the sea."
    C. "Remember," said the father, "never fly very low or very high."
    D. "You can probably guess what happened next."

4. How would you best describe the narrator in both Passage 1 and Passage 2?
    A. a friend
    B. the Scarecrow
    C. an outside observer
    D. the mythical god

5. What conclusion can be drawn about the author's point of view in Passage 2? How does it relate to the theme? Support your answer with details from the text.

_____
_____
_____
_____
_____

28 READING: LITERATURE

6. An author often uses a point of view called omniscient when the narrator tells the reader what characters are thinking or feeling. Fill in the chart with examples of how the author uses an omniscient point of view in Passage 1 and Passage 2.

"The Wonderful Wizard of Oz"	"The Myth of Icarus and Daedelus"

7. How does the narrator develop Icarus' character in Passage 2?
   A. The narrator shows that Icarus is stubborn and refuses to listen to his father.
   B. The narrator develops Icarus as an evil character.
   C. The narrator presents Icarus as a sympathetic character who we should feel sorry for.
   D. The narrator reveals Icarus' youth and carelessness, which leads to his death.

8. How would Passage 1 (Excerpt from Wonderful Wizard of Oz) change if the story was told from another point of view? Describe the effect on the reader if the point of view changed.

_____
_____
_____
_____

9. Re-read Passage 2 (Excerpt from The Myth of Icarus and Daedelus). Now, rewrite the story from a first person point of view.

_____
_____
_____
_____
_____
_____

READING: LITERATURE

29

USE IMAGES TO UNDERSTAND TEXT

RL.4.7 Make connections between the text of a story or drama and a visual or oral presentation of the text, identifying where each version reflects specific descriptions and directions in the text.

Directions: Read the passage and answer the questions below.

Passage 1: Mouse Deer and Tiger

Mouse Deer sang his song as he walked through the forest. He was looking for tasty fruits and roots and shoots. Although he was small, he wasn't afraid of the other bigger animals who wanted to eat him

Then he heard something. Rowr!

There was Tiger!

"Hello, Mouse Deer. I was just getting hungry. Now you can be my lunch."

Mouse Deer didn't want to be lunch. He looked around and thought fast. He saw a mud puddle.

"I'm sorry, Tiger. I can't be your lunch. The King has ordered me to guard his pudding."

"His pudding?" said Tiger.

"Yes. There it is." Mouse Deer pointed to the mud puddle. "It has the best taste in the world. The King doesn't want anyone else to eat it."

Tiger looked longingly at the puddle. "I would like to taste the King's pudding."

"Oh, no, Tiger! The King would be very angry."

"Just one little taste, Mouse Deer! The King will never know."

"Well, all right, Tiger. But first let me run far away, so no one will blame me."

"All right, Mouse Deer, you can go now."

Mouse Deer ran quickly out of sight.

"Imagine!" said Tiger. "The King's pudding!" He took a big mouthful.

Phooey! He spit it out.

"Yuck! Ugh! Bleck! That's no pudding. That's mud!"

Tiger ran through the forest. He caught up with Mouse Deer.

READING: LITERATURE

"Mouse Deer, you tricked me once. But now you will be my lunch!"

Mouse Deer looked around and thought fast. He saw a wasp nest in a tree.

"I'm sorry, Tiger. I can't be your lunch. The King has ordered me to guard his drum."

"His drum?" said Tiger.

"Yes. There it is." Mouse Deer pointed to the wasp nest. "It has the best sound in the world. The King doesn't want anyone else to hit it."

Tiger said, "I would like to hit the King's drum."

"Oh, no, Tiger! The King would be very angry."

"Just one little hit, Mouse Deer! The King will never know."

"Well, all right, Tiger. But first let me run far away, so no one will blame me."

"All right, Mouse Deer, you can go now."

Mouse Deer ran quickly out of sight.

"Imagine!" said Tiger. "The King's drum!" He reached up and hit it. The wasps all flew out. They started to sting Tiger.

"Ouch! That's no drum. That's a wasp nest!"

Tiger ran away. But the wasps only followed him!

Tiger came to a stream. He jumped in and stayed underwater as long as he could. At last the wasps went away.

Then Tiger jumped out. He ran through the forest till he found Mouse Deer.

"Mouse Deer, you tricked me once. You tricked me twice. But now you will be my lunch!"

Mouse Deer looked around and thought fast. He saw a cobra! The giant snake was coiled asleep on the ground.

"I'm sorry, Tiger. I can't be your lunch. The King has ordered me to guard his belt."

"His belt?" said Tiger.

"Yes. There it is." Mouse Deer pointed to the cobra. "It's the best belt in the world. The King doesn't want anyone else to wear it."

Tiger said, "I would like to wear the King's belt."

"Oh, no Tiger! The King would be very angry."

"Just for one moment, Mouse Deer! The King will never know."

"Well, all right, Tiger. But first let me run far away, so no one will blame me."

"All right, Mouse Deer, you can go now."

Mouse Deer ran quickly out of sight.

"Imagine!" said Tiger. "The King's belt!" He started to wrap it around himself.

The cobra woke up. It didn't wait for Tiger to finish wrapping. It wrapped itself around Tiger. Then it squeezed him and bit him.

"Ooh! Ow! Yow! That's no belt. That's a cobra! Help! Mouse Deer! Help!"

But Mouse Deer was far away. And as he went, he sang his song.

1. The following question has two parts. First answer Part A. Then, answer Part B.

Part A

Read the passage "Mouse Deer and Tiger." Then view the book cover of a different version of this story. Which statement best explains the connection between the passage and illustration?

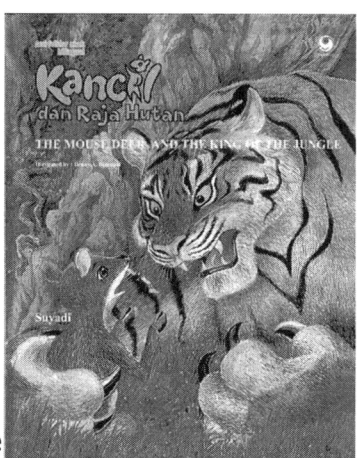

A. The passage which describes how the Mouse Deer outsmarts the Tiger, and the illustration reinforces this.
B. The passage which describes the Tiger's intent to eat the Mouse Deer, and the illustration reinforces this idea.
C. The passage which describes how the animals become best friends, and the illustration supports this idea.
D. The passage which describes a rivalry between the Mouse Deer and the Tiger, but the illustration does not support this.

Part B

Which piece of evidence from the passage **best** supports the comparison statement in Part A?

A. "Hello, Mouse Deer. I was just getting hungry. Now you can be my lunch."
B. "Tiger ran through the forest. He caught up with Mouse Deer."
C. "Although he was small, he wasn't afraid of the other bigger animals who wanted to eat him."
D. "He jumped in and stayed underwater as long as he could. At last the wasps went away."

2. Look at the illustration in question 1 again. Which of the statements below is the most accurate description of the illustration in relation to Passage 1?
   A. The illustration does not represent the passage. While it shows the Mouse Deer and the Tiger, it does not accurately represent the way the characters look according to the text.
   B. The illustration does represent the passage. It shows the Mouse Deer and the Tiger, with the tiger in control of the situation and frightening the Mouse Deer.
   C. The illustration does not fully represent the passage. While it does show the Tiger trying to capture the Mouse Deer, it does not show how cleverly the Mouse Deer tricks the Tiger, which is a major event in the story.
   D. The illustration does represent the passage. It shows the main idea that the Tiger is the king of the forest and all the other animals must follow his lead.

3. The following question has two parts. First answer Part A. Then, answer Part B.

Part A
Select a moral for this story.
   A. Be happy with who you are.
   B. Cleverness is more important than size.
   C. Kindness is always the most important thing.
   D. Cheaters never win.

Part B
Does the illustration in question 1 support the moral?
   A. No, because it doesn't show how much bigger the tiger is.
   B. No, because it doesn't convey the cleverness of the deer mouse.
   C. Yes, because it shows that the tiger can't win by cheating.
   D. Yes, because it reveals that even different creatures can be friends.

4. What do you think an illustration that captures the main idea of this story would show? Support your answer with evidence from the text.

_____

_____

_____

_____

_____

READING: LITERATURE   33

Passage 2: The Little Red Hen, an English Folk Tale

1   A Little Red Hen lived in a barnyard. She spent almost all of her time walking about the barnyard in her picketty-pecketty fashion, scratching everywhere for worms. She dearly loved fat, delicious worms and felt they were absolutely necessary to the health of her children.

2   A cat usually napped lazily in the barn door, not even bothering herself to scare the rat who ran here and there as he pleased. And as for the pig who lived in the sty — he did not care what happened so long as he could eat and grow fat.

3   One day the Little Red Hen found a seed. It was a wheat seed, but the Little Red Hen was so accustomed to bugs and worms that she supposed this to be some new and perhaps very delicious kind of meat. Carrying it about, she made many inquiries as to what it might be. She found it was a wheat seed and that, if planted, it would grow up, and when ripe, it could be made into flour and then into bread.

4   When she discovered that, she knew it ought to be planted. However, she was so busy hunting food for herself and her family that, naturally, she thought she ought not to take time to plant it. So she thought of the Pig — upon whom time must hang heavily and of the Cat who had nothing to do, and of the great fat Rat with his idle hours, and she called loudly: "Who will plant the seed?" But the Pig said, "Not I," and the Cat said, "Not I," and the Rat said, "Not I." "Well, then," said the Little Red Hen, "I will." And she did.

5   Then she went on with her daily duties through the long summer days, scratching for worms and feeding her chicks, while the Pig grew fat, and the Cat grew fat, and the Rat grew fat, and the wheat grew tall and ready for harvest. So one day the Little Red Hen chanced to notice how large the wheat was and that the grain was ripe, so she ran about calling briskly: "Who will cut the wheat?" The Pig said, "Not I," the Cat said, "Not I," and the Rat said, "Not I." "Well, then," said the Little Red Hen, "I will." And she did.

6   She got the sickle from among the farmer's tools in the barn and proceeded to cut off all of the big plant of wheat. On the ground lay the nicely cut wheat, ready to be gathered and threshed, but the newest and yellowest and downiest of Mrs. Hen's chicks set up a "peep-peep-peeping" in their most vigorous fashion, proclaiming to the world at large, but most particularly to their mother, that she was neglecting them.

7   Poor Little Red Hen! She felt quite bewildered and hardly knew where to turn. Her attention was sorely divided between her duty to her children and her duty to the wheat, for which she felt responsible. So, again, in a very hopeful tone, she called out, "Who will thresh the wheat?" But the Pig, with a grunt, said, "Not I," and the Cat, with a meow, said, "Not I," and the Rat, with a squeak, said, "Not I." So the Little Red Hen, looking, it must be admitted, rather discouraged, said, "Well, I will, then." And she did.

8   Of course, she had to feed her babies first, though, and when she had gotten them all to sleep for their afternoon nap, she went out and threshed the wheat.

9   After this really strenuous day Mrs. Hen retired to her slumbers earlier than usual. She would have liked to sleep late in the morning, but her chicks, joining in the morning chorus of the hen yard, drove away all hopes of such a luxury. Even as she sleepily half opened one eye, the thought came to her that to-day that wheat must, somehow, be made into bread. She was not in the habit of making bread, although, of course, anyone can make it if he or she follows the recipe with care, and she knew perfectly well that she could do it if necessary.

10   So after her children were fed and made sweet and fresh for the day, she hunted up the Pig, the Cat and the Rat. Still confident that they would surely help her some day she sang out, "Who will make the bread?" Alas for the Little Red Hen! Once more her hopes were dashed! For the Pig said, "Not I," the Cat said, "Not I," and the Rat said, "Not I." So the Little Red Hen said once more, "I will then," and she did.

11   At last the great moment arrived. A delicious odor was wafted upon the autumn breeze. The Red Hen did not know whether the bread would be fit to eat, but — joy of joys! — when the lovely brown loaves came out of the oven, they were done to perfection. Then, probably because she had acquired the habit, the Red Hen called: "Who will eat the bread?" All the animals in the barnyard were watching hungrily and smacking their lips in anticipation, and the Pig said, "I will," the Cat said, "I will," the Rat said, "I will."

12   But the Little Red Hen said, "No, you won't. I will." And she did.

5. View the image next to this question. How does the image compare to the text?

    A. The image illustrates the text's account of the hen doing work while the other animals sleep or watch.
    B. The image shows the Little Red Hen escaping to a different farm.
    C. The image represents the text well because it shows the hen asleep.
    D. The image shows why the Little Red Hen likes looking for worms and seeds.

6. View the image below. Identify the part of the text that describes the illustration.
   A. "All the animals in the barnyard were watching hungrily and smacking their lips in anticipation, and the Pig said, "I will," the Cat said, "I will," the Rat said, "I will."
   B. "She got the sickle from among the farmer's tools in the barn and proceeded to cut off all of the big plant of wheat".
   C. "Poor Little Red Hen! She felt quite bewildered and hardly knew where to turn. Her attention was sorely divided between her duty to her children and her duty to the wheat, for which she felt responsible."
   D. "She spent almost all of her time walking about the barnyard in her picketty-pecketty fashion, scratching everywhere for worms."

7. View the following image of Disney's adaptation of the story, "The Wise Little Hen." Does the illustration represent Passage 2 "The Little Red Hen?"
   A. Yes, because it has the same characters.
   B. Yes, because the text and the image both show how much the hen has to do.
   C. No, because the image doesn't show the frustration the hen faced when the other animals refused to work.
   D. No, because the setting of the text and the movie are different.

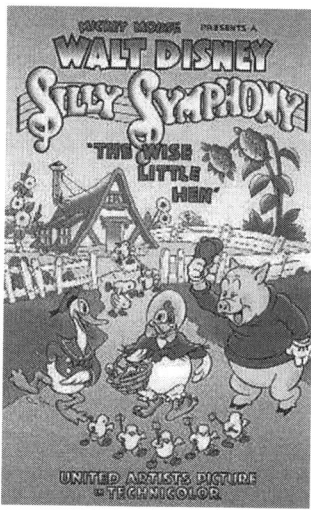

8. What would you identify as the moral of this text? Which of the images (from question 5, 6, or 7) **best** represents this moral? Use evidence from the text to support your answer.

_____

_____

_____

_____

READING: LITERATURE

COMPARE & CONTRAST THEMES/ EVENTS IN DIFFERENT CULTURAL STORIES/ MYTHS

RL.4.9 Compare and contrast the treatment of similar themes and topics (opposition or good and evil) and patterns of events (the quest) in stories, myths, and traditional literature from different cultures.

Directions: Read the passages and answer the questions below.

Passage 1 : "The Donkey, The Fox, and the Lion"
by Aesop

The Donkey and the Fox, having entered into partnership together for their mutual protection, went out into the forest to hunt. They had not proceeded far when they met a Lion. The Fox, seeing imminent danger, approached the Lion and promised to contrive for him the capture of the Donkey if the Lion would pledge his word not to harm the Fox. Then, upon assuring the Donkey that he would not be injured, the Fox led him to a deep pit and arranged that he should fall into it. The Lion, seeing that the Donkey was secured, immediately pounced on the Fox and attacked the Donkey.

Passage 2: "The Fox and the Crow"
by Aesop

1   The fox once saw a crow fly by with a piece of cheese in her beak. "I want that cheese," thought the fox.

2   He sat down beneath the tree and called, "Good day, Miss Crow. How well you are looking, how bright your eyes, how glossy your feathers." The crow was pleased. She loved to be flattered.

3   "I am sure your voice is even more beautiful than your feathers," cried the Fox.

4   "Won't you sing a song for me, O queen of the birds?"

5   The crow was so pleased that she could hardly sit still.

6   She lifted her head high, closed her eyes and opened her beak to sing. "Cawwww!"

7   The cheese fell to the ground right in front of the fox.

8   "Thank you Miss Crow," he said to the unhappy bird. "In exchange for your cheese, I will give one piece of advice: never trust a flatterer."

1. What theme is developed in Passage 1?
   A. Betraying a friend has consequences.
   B. There is no such thing as a true friendship.
   C. Animals never protect each other.
   D. True friends never leave one another.

2. What is a theme of both Passages 1 and 2?
   A. Hard work is rewarded.
   B. Foxes are not smart.
   C. Don't let your guard down.
   D. There is strength in numbers.

3. What is the main theme of Passage 2?
   A. Foxes are too lazy to get their own food.
   B. Don't trust a stranger's flattery.
   C. Crows are not smart.
   D. Stealing food from birds is easy.

4. Read Passages 1 and 2. Match the statements to compare how Aesop approaches the topic of deception in each text.
   - Aesop has a character explicitly address the topic of deception by stating the moral.
   - Aesop uses the actions of multiple characters to explore the topic of deception.

"The Donkey, The Fox, and the Lion"	"The Fox and the Crow"

5. What text structure does Aesop use to develop his topic in both passages?
   A. In "The Donkey, The Fox, and the Lion" the author uses first person narration, while in "The Fox and the Crow" the author uses setting.
   B. In "The Donkey, The Fox, and the Lion" the author uses third person narration, while in "The Fox and the Crow" the author uses dialogue.
   C. In "The Donkey, The Fox, and the Lion" the author uses characters, while in "The Fox and the Crow" the author uses setting.
   D. In "The Donkey, The Fox, and the Lion" the author uses first person narration, while in "The Fox and the Crow" the author uses dialogue.

READING: LITERATURE

6. How are the patterns of events in Passages 1 and 2 similar?

Passage 3: Excerpt from "The Three Little Pigs"
by Joseph Jacobs

At the beginning of this story, the wolf is trying to eat the pig.

1   The next day the wolf came again, and said to the little pig, "Little pig, there is a fair at Shanklin this afternoon. Will you go?"

2   "Oh yes," said the pig, "I will go. What time shall you be ready?"

3   "At three," said the wolf. So the little pig set off before the time as usual, and got to the fair, and bought a butter churn, which he was going home with, when he saw the wolf coming. He did not know what to do, so he got into the churn to hide, and by so doing turned it around, and it rolled down the hill with the pig in it. This frightened the wolf so much that he ran home without going to the fair. He went to the pig's house, and told him how frightened he had been by a great round thing which came down the hill past him.

4   Then the little pig said, "Ha, I frightened you, then. I had been to the fair and bought a butter churn, and when I saw you, I got into it, and rolled down the hill."

5   Then the wolf was very angry indeed, and declared he would eat up the little pig, and that he would get down the chimney after him. When the little pig saw what he was about, he hung up the pot full of water, and made a blazing fire, and, just as the wolf was coming down, took off the cover, and in fell the wolf. The little pig put on the cover again in an instant, boiled him up, and ate him for supper, and lived happily ever afterwards.

7. The following question has two parts. First answer Part A. Then, answer Part B.

Part A
What is the theme of Passage 3?
  A. Working hard is the most important quality.
  B. The best way to target a bully is to ignore him.
  C. Using fear can help you outsmart an enemy.
  D. Deception has consequences.

Part B

Which statement from the text best supports the answer in Part A?

    A. "So the little pig went off before the time as usual, and got to the fair, and bought a butter churn…"

    B. "Then the wolf was very angry indeed, and declared he would eat up the little pig, and that he would get down the chimney after him."

    C. "He did not know what to do, so he got into the churn to hide, and by so doing turned it around, and it rolled down the hill with the pig in it."

    D. "Little pig, there is a fair at Shanklin this afternoon. Will you go?"

8. How does the theme in "The Three Little Pigs" relate to the themes in Passages 1 and 2?

READING: INFORMATION

UNDERSTAND TEXT

RI.4.1 Refer to details and examples in a text when explaining what the text says explicitly and when drawing inferences from the text.

Directions: Read the passage and answer the questions below.

Passage 1: Humpback Whales

1   Humpback whales are mammals found in most of the world's oceans. Like many whales, they are endangered. The species was hunted by commercial "whalers" in the north Pacific Ocean for many years. This almost led to its extinction. In 1966 a new law made killing whales for sport or profit illegal. By that time, only about 1400 humpbacks existed. Since then, the humpback population has increased.

2   A humpback whale is easy to identify because of its stocky body and hump. Its head and mouth are covered by knobby hair follicles called tubercles. The humpback is known for its size, averaging 40-50 ft long. Females are typically larger than males. Humpbacks eat krill and small fish.

3   One feature of humpbacks is a behavior they do when they come to the surface of the ocean called breaching. When a whale breaches, it jumps out of the water. Not only does this allow the whale to breathe, scientists think it may be a social action. Breaching makes humpbacks a favorite of whale watchers.

4   Humpbacks also produce a complex song. Both females and males make sounds. But only males "sing" a long, loud song that can last up to 20 minutes. He may then repeat it for hours. Although scientists don't know exactly why the humpback sings, they believe it may be related to attracting mates, to showing authority over other male whales, or echolocation to find and identify food.

1. Based on the information in the text, which is a unique feature of humpback whales?
    - **A.** The males are large.
    - **B.** They are endangered.
    - **C.** They jump out of the water.
    - **D.** They hunt prey.

2. Why was the law in 1966 important?
    - **A.** It likely kept humpbacks from becoming extinct.
    - **B.** It made people start protesting that whales should not be killed for sport.
    - **C.** It caused a decrease in the humpback whale population.
    - **D.** It led to the discovery of why humpbacks sing.

3. Which of the following is NOT a possible reason for the humpback's song?

   A. The humpback male sings to show power over the other males.

   B. It helps the humpback find food.

   C. The song attracts females to the male whale.

   D. It scares away predators.

4. Name three characteristics that describe a humpback whale. Give evidence from the text to support your answer.

   _____

   _____

   _____

   _____

Passage 2: The Song of the Humpback

1	Male humpback whales are known for their long, loud melodies. Humpback songs can be heard over 100 miles away. They don't have vocal chords, but sing through their noses. These so-called songs are especially common in breeding season, when whales are looking for females to mate with so they can have baby whales. The entire song lasts anywhere from 10 to 20 minutes, and then the whale may repeat it over and over for hours.

2	These songs have more in common with a musical composition than you might expect. The humpback's song isn't just a random set of sounds. Instead, the song contains repeated patterns. As the whale repeats a pattern, he changes it. The song develops and changes over time.

3	Scientists have now discovered that humpbacks create a new song every year. Sometimes this is an entirely new creation. Other times, the whales will borrow parts of the previous year's song. Sometimes, they combine verses from old and new songs. The whales can switch mid-song between old and new at points where songs sound the same.

4	Whales from the same family community, or pod, sing the same song. Members of nearby pods may produce songs that are the same or similar. In fact, researchers traced one song all the way from whales in Australia to French Polynesia. They believe the song traveled from pod to pod across 4,000 miles! This is a major discovery in whale behavior. It shows that, like humans, whales exchange culture (learned behaviors) with one another.

5. The songs of male humpback whales are
    A. a random set of sounds.
    B. sung over and over.
    C. repeated by female whales.
    D. difficult to hear.

6. How are whales like humans?
    A. Their population is growing, like humans.
    B. Whale sounds can be heard as far away as human sounds.
    C. Whale songs show that music is a language understood by all.
    D. Like humans, the passing on of whale songs shows how whales share culture.

7. The following question has two parts. First answer Part A. Then, answer Part B.

Part A

Which factor is most important for when a humpback whale switches between old and new songs?

    A. parts where the songs sound similar
    B. how far the song has traveled
    C. the process is random
    D. the whale is trying to find a new mate

Part B

Which detail from the text supports the answer for Part A?

    A. "The song develops and changes over time."
    B. "The whales can switch mid-song between old and new at points where songs sound the same."
    C. "Scientists have now discovered that humpbacks create a new song every year."
    D. "These songs have more in common with a musical composition than you might think."

8. How are the songs of humpback whales shared across long distances? Use evidence from the text to support your answer.

DETERMINE MAIN IDEA & SUMMARIZE TEXT

RI.4.2 Determine the main idea of a text and explain how it is supported by key details; summarize the text.

Directions: Read the passage and answer the questions below.

Passage 1: The Greatest Swimmer of All

1   Michael Phelps is an American swimmer and champion. He has won more Olympic gold medals than anyone else in history. He competed in 5 Olympics and won gold medals in 4 Olympic Games in a row.

2   Michael's body helps him swim well. He is tall, with a long thin torso and shorter legs. His arms are very long, 6 feet 7 inches across from fingertip to fingertip. His arms act like paddles to propel him through the water. His size 14 feet are also large, and act like flippers in the water. And though his body is built for swimming, Michael worked hard for 17 years to be the best.

3   Michael retired in 2016 and didn't plan to race again. But the Discovery Channel asked him to promote Shark Week by racing a great white shark. Michael practiced for his race by racing against computer-generated reef and hammerhead sharks. On July 23, 2017, Michael Phelps faced a computer-generated great white shark. Michael swam in the pool, while the film crew inserted video of his opponent in the Atlantic Ocean.

4   A great white shark is able to swim 25 miles per hour for short amounts of time. Michael has endurance, meaning he can swim well for a long time. But although he wore a special wetsuit, Michael was no match for the shark. Michael swam 100 meters in an impressive 38.1 seconds, but the shark was faster. The shark covered the distance in 36.1 seconds. Although Michael playfully asked for a rematch, he admitted that there was "probably very little chance for me to beat him [the shark]." So who is the greatest swimmer of all time? It seems the great white shark may be the king of the seas!

1. What is the main idea of paragraph 2?
   A. Michael Phelps is is a better swimmer than a great white shark.
   B. Michael Phelps's body shape helps him be a great swimmer.
   C. Michael Phelps is the best Olympian ever.
   D. Michael Phelps has big feet that act like flippers in the water.

2. Which detail from the text best supports the title "The Greatest Swimmer of All"?
   A. "It seems the great white shark may be the king of the seas!"
   B. "And though his body is built for swimming, Michael worked hard for 17 years to be the best."
   C. "He has won more Olympic gold medals than anyone else in history."
   D. "Michael practiced for his race by racing against computer-generated reef and hammerhead sharks."

3. **Part A.**
What is the main idea in the text?
   A. The great white shark swims faster than Michael Phelps
   B. The Discovery Channel promoted Shark Week by racing a great white shark against Michael Phelps.
   C. Michael Phelps came out of retirement to race against a shark.
   D. Michael Phelps worked very hard to be the fastest swimmer in the world

Part B
Which of the following is NOT a supporting detail of that main idea?
   A. "But although he wore a special wetsuit, Michael was no match for the shark."
   B. "Although Michael playfully asked for a rematch, he admitted that there was 'probably very little chance for me to beat him [the shark].'"
   C. "Michael swam 100 meters in an impressive 38.1 seconds, but the shark was faster."
   D. "Michael swam in the pool, while the film crew inserted video of his opponent in the Atlantic Ocean."

4. Summarize the text from beginning to end in a few sentences.

Passage 2: Practice Makes Permanent

1   Every 4 years, the best athletes in the world compete for gold at the Olympics. But how does an athlete become the best of the best? Training to be a great athlete may be different that you expect. Fans usually only see exciting competitions. They don't see the hours that go into training an athlete's body and mind. Athletes at the top of their sport dedicate their lives to trying to win.

2   Becoming the best in a sport involves more than just showing up at the gym every day. Athletes who want to rise to the top must commit. Training is a way of life for them. In training their bodies, athletes must build up flexibility, balance, and muscle strength. They must have the endurance to keep going.

3   Athletes must also prepare for distractions like noise and pressure. This helps them overcome distractions in competition. The best athletes can turn nervousness into positive energy. They rely on their training to get through tough competitions. Rather than think about every step, a well-trained athlete can be "in the zone." Their body knows exactly what to do from hours of practice.

4   Why can't athletes just practice their skills during competition? If an athlete wants to improve, it's important to practice over and over without the pressure of winning. In practice, he or she can concentrate on specific moves or skills. This builds muscle memory, where the athlete's body just knows what to do. During a competition, an athlete must be confident that those skills are mastered. Olympic athletes make a commitment to be the best they can be. Practice makes not only perfect, but permanent.

5. What is the main idea of this article?
    A. Top athletes must train their bodies and minds to become the best.
    B. Most athletes don't like to practice.
    C. Athletes must prepare for distractions and noise in competition.
    D. Athletes train to be fast and strong so that fans can expect an exciting competition when they perform.

6. According to the article, why do athletes prepare for distractions?
    A. to be "in the zone" during practice
    B. to help them be better than their competitors
    C. to learn to stay focused on what skills they still need to learn
    D. to make sure they are ready for unusual distractions during competition

7. The following question has two parts. First answer Part A. Then, answer Part B.

Part A

Which factor is most important for muscle memory?
- A. distractions like noise
- B. practicing a skill over and over
- C. being in a competition under pressure
- D. confidence

Part B

Which detail from the text supports the answer for Part A?
- A. "Becoming the best in a sport involves more than just showing up at the gym every day."
- B. "If an athlete wants to improve, it's important to practice over and over without the pressure of winning."
- C. "Olympic athletes make a commitment to be the best they can be."
- D. "The best athletes can turn nervousness into positive energy."

8. Based on details in the article, what does "Practice makes not only perfect, but permanent" mean? Use evidence from the text to support your answer.

_____

_____

_____

_____

_____

USE DETAILS TO EXPLAIN EVENTS, PROCEDURES & IDEAS IN TEXT

RI.4.3 Explain events, procedures, ideas, or concepts in a historical, scientific, or technical text, including what happened and why, based on specific information in the text

Directions: Read the passage and answer the questions below.

Passage 1: Betsy Ross and the American Flag

1   Betsy Ross was born in Pennsylvania on January 1, 1752. She lived during the Revolutionary war in America. Her birthname was Elizabeth Griscom, but she went by Betsy. After completing basic schooling, she became an apprentice (someone who works for a skilled or qualified person in order to learn a trade) in a sewing shop. She learned about the sewing trade and met John Ross, who she would later marry. Betsy and John's families did not approve of the marriage because they were from different churches. Betsy was cut off from her Quaker family and joined John's church, where future president George Washington attended.

2   Betsy and John started their own upholstery, or sewing, business. Shortly after, the Revolutionary War started in America. It was hard for the sewing business to get fabric. Business was slow. With their business struggling, John joined the war. In January 1776 John Ross was killed in an explosion. He died days later.

3   Later in 1776, Betsy met with the Committee of Three. George Washington, George Ross, and Robert Morris were members of a secret committee. The men asked her to sew the first American flag. In Betsy's story, General Washington showed her a rough design of the flag. The flag would show unity against Britain in the war. According to Betsy, the flag was finished by June 1776. In July the Declaration of Independence was signed. A new nation was born: America.

4   The flag was officially adopted in 1777. It was a symbol of national unity and pride. Like the new country, Betsy's life was far from easy. She was married twice more, but her husbands died before her. Two of her children died. She lived a long life and died at the age of 84 on January 30, 1836.

1. What happened just after the first flag was finished?
   - **A.** The Declaration of Independence was signed.
   - **B.** George Washington asked for Betsy Ross's help.
   - **C.** Betsy Ross was married again.
   - **D.** The flag was officially adopted.

2. Why did John Ross join the war?
   - **A.** He believed in its cause.
   - **B.** The sewing business was slow due to lack of fabric.
   - **C.** The sewing business wasn't something he wanted to do.
   - **D.** He thought Betsy should become a nurse.

3. What was a result of Betsy and John's marriage?
   - **A.** Betsy had a difficult life.
   - **B.** John joined the war to provide money for his new wife.
   - **C.** Betsy was rejected by her church and family.
   - **D.** Betsy learned about the sewing trade.

4. Think about two historical events: the sewing of the first flag, and the signing of the Declaration of Independence. Explain how they are connected. Give evidence from the text to support your answer.

_____

_____

_____

_____

_____

_____

Passage 2: Video Game Production

1   Have you ever thought about how your favorite video game was created? This depends on the specific game, but the basic process is the same for most games. Making a video game is a complicated, exciting task.

2   A video game begins with an idea. Ideas can come from well-known stories, characters, or may be made up. Next, a preproduction team is made. This team usually has a director, designer, engineer, artist, and writer. Each member is important. The team writes the game's story and how it will work. They decide how the game will be played and what technology will be needed.

3   Next storyboards are drawn by the artist. Each storyboard describes a scene in the game. Then, designers map out each level of play. This includes all of the different worlds a player will move through in the game.

4   After the storyboards and game designs are complete, production begins. Engineers and computer programmers write "code," a language that computers understand. Some animated games use 3D models. The game's outline is now ready. With the basics of the game set, the production team tries to make it perfect. Special effects are added.

5   After production is finished, the game goes to postproduction. Users test the first version. The engineer uses technology to fix issues. This makes the product as good as possible. Now the final product is ready to be released. Finally, the game can be bought in stores and online. Many people see this as the beginning of a game's life. Little do they know it's actually the middle of a long journey!

5. What happens right after production is finished (when postproduction begins).
    A. Users rate the game as good or bad.
    B. The game is sold online.
    C. Users test the game.
    D. The game is given special effects.

6. Which task is NOT the job of the preproduction team?
    A. The team sells the game to buyers.
    B. The team develops the story.
    C. The team creates storyboards.
    D. The team decides what technology the game needs.

7. The following question has two parts. First answer Part A. Then, answer Part B.

Part A

Why is it important to test the game before release?
- A. so that the game can be improved, if needed
- B. so that the production team can see if people like it
- C. so that customers can decide if they want to buy it
- D. so that the preproduction team can decide whether to make another game in the series

Part B

Which detail from the text supports the answer for Part A?
- A. "After production is finished, the game goes to postproduction."
- B. "The engineer uses technology to fix issues. This makes the product as good as possible."
- C. "Finally, the game can be bought in stores and online."
- D. "They decide how the game will be played and what technology will be needed."

8. Explain the production phase of creating a video game. Use information from the text in your explanation.

DETERMINE WORD MEANING IN TEXT

RI.4.4 Determine the meaning of general academic and domain-specific words or phrases in a text relevant to a grade 4 topic or subject area.

Directions: Read the passage and answer the questions below.

Passage 1: Fennec Foxes in the Desert

    1   Fennec foxes lives in the Sahara Desert. At about 3 pounds the fennec fox is the smallest fox in the world, but you wouldn't know it by looking at its six-inch ears.

    2   Fennec foxes are most recognized for their large, bat-like ears. Those ears aren't just for hearing, they're actually a way of survival. The tiny foxes must survive in the sweltering heat of the desert, where the daytime temperature can go over 100 degrees. Their huge ears radiate heat away from their body to help keep them cool.

    3   Fennec foxes are very adaptive. Aside from their ears, they have several other characteristics that help them thrive in the harsh desert climate. Their thick hair insulates them. The hair keeps their bodies warm on cold nights. It also protects them from the sun on hot days. Their nocturnal habits also help fennec foxes avoid the searing heat of the desert during the day. Finally, their hairy feet protect them from the scorching sand.

    4   The foxes' feet also act like shovels. They dig often, making the underground dens where they live. Fennec foxes live in these dens in small communities. They eat what they can find, foraging for plants and eating small mammals and reptiles.

1. What does the word scorching mean in paragraph 3?
   A. hot
   B. desert
   C. cold
   D. prickly

2. What word could be substituted for the word radiate in paragraph 2?
   A. measure
   B. release
   C. cover
   D. squirt

3. What does nocturnal mean?
   A. fearful
   B. eats plants and animals
   C. hunts during the day
   D. active at night

4. Why do you think the author used the word 'adaptive' to describe fennec foxes? Give evidence from the text to support your answer.

_____

_____

_____

_____

_____

Passage 2: Bats in the Night

1   As night falls, the edge of the cave suddenly flutters with movement. And then, out of the cave comes a flurry of creatures flying through the dusky air. One creature's silhouette can be seen in the **twilight**. It's a bird, it's a plane, it's a… bat?

2   Bats are the only mammals that can fly. They are warm-blooded and have hair on their bodies. Baby bats, called pups, feed on their mother's milk. Bats sleep upside down, hanging by their feet, in a roost. But unlike most animals and humans, they sleep during the day and are active at night. Overnight they fly and search for food—they're nocturnal!

3   One reason that bats succeed as nocturnal creatures is through echolocation. Although they can see, they locate food and maneuver in the dark by listening for echoes. The bat produces a high-pitched chirp, and as the sound travels through the air, it listens for echoes. When the chirp hits an object or potential food, the sound bounces off and makes its way back to the bat's sensitive ears. The echo tells the bat how big it is, where its located, and even if it's moving.

4   Some people are afraid of these creatures. But scientists want people to know that bats are shy and **mild** around humans. They can even be helpful! Bats benefit humans in a few ways. They eat insects, which helps keep pesky bugs away from homes. They can eat hundreds of insects in an hour. Some bats eat flower nectar and fruit. They help new plants grow by **distributing** seeds in different places. Because of these benefits, some people even place bat houses in their yards.

5. Reread this sentence from paragraph 2.
"But unlike most animals and humans, they sleep during the day and are active at night."
In the sentence, what does the prefix un- mean in the word unlike?
   - **A.** again
   - **B.** with
   - **C.** not
   - **D.** before

6. Which word has the opposite meaning of the word mild as it is used in paragraph 4?
   - **A.** harsh
   - **B.** gentle
   - **C.** cautious
   - **D.** spicy

7. The following question has two parts. First answer Part A. Then, answer Part B.

Part A

Which of these words is closest to the meaning of the word twilight in paragraph 1?
- **A.** cave
- **B.** air
- **C.** morning
- **D.** sunset

Part B

Which **two** details from the text help the reader understand the meaning of the word twilight in Part A?
- **A.** "As night falls…"
- **B.** "a flurry of creatures"
- **C.** "flying through the dusky air"
- **D.** "…flutters with movement"
- **E.** "It's a bird, it's a plane…"

8. What does the word **distributing** mean in paragraph 4? What strategies can you use to help you find the meaning of the word? Use information from the text in your explanation.

DESCRIBE STRUCTURE OF EVENTS, IDEAS OR INFORMATION IN TEXT

RI.4.5 Describe the overall structure (e.g., chronology, comparison, cause/effect, problem/solution) of events, ideas, concepts, or information in a text or part of a text.

Directions: Read the passage and answer the questions below.

Passage 1: Is It a Cold or Allergies?

1   Achoo! As fall turns to winter, doctor's offices fill up with sneezing patients. Is it a cold? Or could it be allergies? And how can you tell the difference?

The Common Cold

2   A cold is caused by a virus that enters the body through the mouth, eyes, or nose. The virus can spread through droplets in the air when a sick person coughs or sneezes. The virus then infects the nose and throat. A cold may cause a sore throat, runny nose, cough, congestion, and sneezing.

3   Most people have two or three colds each year. There aren't many medicines that help fight a cold virus. The body relies on its immune system to get rid of the virus. The immune system works to defend the body against "attacks" by viruses or bacteria. To support the body, doctors recommend lots of fluids and rest during a cold.

Allergies

4   Allergies may seem similar to a cold, but the causes are very different. An allergy occurs when the body's immune system reacts to something the body comes in contact with. This could be something in the environment, like pollen or mold. It could also be a food, medicine, or insect sting. Allergy symptoms can include watery eyes, runny nose, sneezing, or a rash. Sometimes they even cause trouble breathing.

5   When a person encounters an allergen, their immune system makes an antibody that fights against it. This antibody is what causes symptoms. Unlike a cold, where the body eventually fights off the virus, the body will likely always react to an allergen. Allergies can be much longer lasting than a cold. But, they can be treated by avoiding allergens or with medicines that help the symptoms.

6   So how will you know if you have a cold or allergies? A short-term illness caused by contact with a virus is a cold. Allergies can't be spread from person to person and may last longer than a cold. Neither allergies or a cold are fun to experience, but understanding the differences can help you know how to respond.

1. What causes a cold?
    A. An allergen that the body contacts.
    B. A virus that infects the nose and throat.
    C. The immune system fighting something in the environment.
    D. A sore throat or runny nose.

2. What features in the text help you find information about what you are reading?
    A. Bolded words help the reader understand meanings.
    B. Diagrams label the ideas.
    C. Section headings label the ideas being compared.
    D. The title questions what the text will be about.

3. What is the overall structure of paragraph 6?
    A. compare and contrast
    B. chronological order
    C. cause and effect
    D. problem and solution

4. What concepts are being compared and contrasted? Give evidence from the text to support your answer.

60 READING: INFORMATION

Passage 2: Pelé the Great

1 The name Pelé is nearly always associated with the game of soccer. Pelé was born Edson Arantes do Nascimento on October 23, 1940. He was born in Brazil, a country in South America. His father was a soccer player, and although the family was poor, Pelé showed promise in soccer from a young age. As a boy he would kick a rolled-up stocking filled with rags in place of a soccer ball.

2 Pelé showed so much talent that he tried out and earned a spot as a forward on the Santos professional soccer club in 1958 when he was only 15 years old. He scored his first professional goal before he turned 16. Soon, he was asked to play on Brazil's national team. At 17 years old, Pelé led his team to victory in the 1958 World Cup, which is the international soccer championship.

3 Pelé continued to win. He played for two more winning World Cup teams in 1962 and 1970. Pele's header against Italy in the 1970 World Cup final was his teams 100th World Cup goal. Pelé was officially the biggest goal-scorer in the history of soccer. Pelé retired from soccer in 1974. But in 1975 he came out of retirement to join the New York Cosmos, a U.S. soccer team. He led them to a championship in 1977 and retired again.

4 Although Pelé stopped playing soccer, he remains a legend. He became an ambassador for soccer. He worked to promote peace and understanding through sports. Pelé was named "Co-Player of the Century" by FIFA (International Federation of Association Football). In all, he scored 1,281 goals in 1,363 games of his career. Nearly all soccer players are measured against Pelé's legacy.

5. What structure does the author use to present ideas?
   A. comparing Pelé to other players
   B. chronological order
   C. stating a problem and solution
   D. contrasting Pelé's career with his personal life

6. Place the following events from the text in chronological order:

   A. Pelé was born into a Brazilian family.   1._____

   B. Pelé came out of retirement.   2._____

   C. Pelé won his first World Cup.   3._____

   D. Pelé joined his first professional soccer team. 4._____

   E. Pelé retired for the first time.   5._____

   F. Pelé became the biggest goal-scorer in history. 6._____

7. The following question has two parts. First answer Part A. Then, answer Part B.

Part A

What was a result of Pelé's second retirement?
- **A.** Pelé was replaced as the best player in the world.
- **B.** Pelé was forgotten in the world of modern soccer.
- **C.** Pelé changed from being only a player to having an ambassador role.
- **D.** Other players also met Pelé's impressive achievements.

Part B

Which detail from the text supports the answer in Part A?
- **A.** "In all, he scored 1,281 goals in 1,363 games of his career."
- **B.** "But in 1975 he came out of retirement to join the New York Cosmos, a U.S. soccer team."
- **C.** "He was officially the biggest goal-scorer in the history of soccer."
- **D.** "He worked to promote peace and understanding through sports."

8. Describe how this text is organized. Use two specific details from the text to support your answer.

COMPARE & CONTRAST FIRSTHAND & SECONDHAND ACCOUNTS

RI.4.6 Compare and contrast a firsthand and secondhand account of the same event or topic; describe the differences in focus and the information provided.

Directions: Read the passage and answer the questions below.

Passage 1: Excerpt from The Story of My Life
by Helen Keller

1   One day, while I was playing with my new doll, Miss Sullivan put my big rag doll into my lap also, spelled "d-o-l-l" and tried to make me understand that "d-o-l-l" applied to both. Earlier in the day we had had a tussle over the words "m-u-g" and "w-a-t-e-r." Miss Sullivan had tried to impress it upon me that "m-u-g" is mug and that "w-a-t-e-r" is water, but I persisted in confounding the two. In despair she had dropped the subject for the time, only to renew it at the first opportunity. I became impatient at her repeated attempts and, seizing the new doll, I dashed it upon the floor. I was keenly delighted when I felt the fragments of the broken doll at my feet. Neither sorrow nor regret followed my passionate outburst. I had not loved the doll. In the still, dark world in which I lived there was no strong sentiment or tenderness. I felt my teacher sweep the fragments to one side of the hearth, and I had a sense of satisfaction that the cause of my discomfort was removed. She brought me my hat, and I knew I was going out into the warm sunshine. This thought, if a wordless sensation may be called a thought, made me hop and skip with pleasure.

2   We walked down the path to the well-house, attracted by the fragrance of the honeysuckle with which it was covered. Some one was drawing water and my teacher placed my hand under the spout. As the cool stream gushed over one hand she spelled into the other the word water, first slowly, then rapidly. I stood still, my whole attention fixed upon the motions of her fingers. Suddenly I felt a misty consciousness as of something forgotten—a thrill of returning thought; and somehow the mystery of language was revealed to me. I knew then that "w-a-t-e-r" meant the wonderful cool something that was flowing over my hand. That living word awakened my soul, gave it light, hope, joy, set it free! There were barriers still, it is true, but barriers that could in time be swept away.

READING: INFORMATION   63

Passage 2: Unlocking Her World

1   When Anne Sullivan arrived at the home of Helen Keller, she found the deaf and blind young girl disconnected from the world around her. Helen had little communication and only slight understanding of her world. She was often out of control. She would kick and scream in raging tantrums. Desperate for help, Helen's parents hired Anne Sullivan from the Perkins Institute of the Blind.

2   Beginning with the word "doll," Sullivan tried to teach her young charge finger spelling. Helen liked the spelling game at first, but then grew defiant of Anne's teaching. Anne could sense that Helen didn't connect the objects to their spelling, but she pressed on.

3   With dramatic difficulty, Anne taught Helen the word "water." The teacher helped her deaf and blind young student understand the connection between the letters and the liquid by taking Helen outside to the water pump. Placing one of Helen's hands under the flowing water, Sullivan spelled out w-a-t-e-r in her other hand. And suddenly, it clicked. Helen understood what her teacher was doing. The spelling game was no longer a game, but the key to understanding her world. By that evening, Helen had learned 30 words.

1. Passage 1 is told as a
    A. firsthand account
    B. secondhand account
    C. secondary account
    D. biography

2. Who is providing the information in Passage 1?
    A. Anne Sullivan
    B. Helen Keller
    C. Helen's mother
    D. an unknown source

3. What is the author emphasizing mostly in the secondhand account (Passage 2)?
    A. the difficulty of being deaf and mute
    B. Anne's inexperience teaching the blind
    C. Helen's unwillingness to learn
    D. the importance of Anne helping Helen understand

4. What detail did the author of Passage 2 provide to show the difference between Helen's perspective and Anne's?
    A. She explains how difficult it was for Anne to help Helen connect spelling to words.
    B. She explains how Anne tried to make spelling fun for Helen.
    C. She gives examples of many different words that Anne tried to teach before Helen understood "water."
    D. She proves that Anne believed in Helen even when Helen had given up on herself.

READING: INFORMATION

5. Explain how the firsthand and secondhand accounts are similar and different. Use details from both accounts in your answer. Give evidence from the text to support your answer.

_____

_____

_____

_____

_____

_____

_____

6. Compare and contrast Passage 1 and Passage 2 by writing the phrases into a Venn Diagram.

Passage 1 | **Both** | **Passage 2**

Answer Bank:
about Helen Keller
background information
describes how Helen learned words
firsthand account
gives facts
secondhand account
shows emotion
single, specific memory

READING: INFORMATION

7. The following question has two parts. First answer Part A. Then, answer Part B.

Part A
What is the effect of the firsthand account told from Helen's perspective?
- **A.** It tells the reader why she disliked Anne Sullivan at first.
- **B.** It shows her emotions regarding the experience of understanding language.
- **C.** It explains the impact that Helen Keller made on the world.
- **D.** It gives facts about the event.

Part B
Which **two** details from the text support the answer in Part A?
- **A.** "Earlier in the day we had had a tussle over the words "m-u-g" and "w-a-t-e-r.""
- **B.** "We walked down the path to the well-house, attracted by the fragrance of the honeysuckle with which it was covered."
- **C.** "This thought, if a wordless sensation may be called a thought, made me hop and skip with pleasure."
- **D.** "That living word awakened my soul, gave it light, hope, joy, set it free!"
- **E.** "There were barriers still, it is true, but barriers that could in time be swept away."

8. Rewrite the account of Helen's first moment of understanding from the firsthand perspective of Anne Sullivan. Use the information provided in the two passages and add some information that would make sense in a firsthand account.

USE IMAGES/DIAGRAMS TO UNDERSTAND TEXT

RI.4.7 Interpret information presented visually, orally, or quantitatively (e.g., in charts, graphs, diagrams, timelines, animations, or interactive elements on Web pages) and explain how the information contributes to an understanding of the text in which it appears.

Directions: Read the passage, study the graph, and answer the questions below.

Passage 1: How Much Sugar?

Toby conducted an experiment to test how much glucose, or sugar, was in various drinks. He followed the procedure below.

1. Pour a small amount of each drink into a small glass beaker. Pour enough that the entire test strip can be covered in the drink.
2. Dip one glucose test strip (obtained from a pharmacy) into each the first liquid. Completely cover the strip's test area.
3. Remove the strip from the liquid and lay it on a solid white background. This will make it easier to see what color the test strip has turned.
4. Wait exactly 30 seconds, then match the color of the test strip to a color-coded chart which measures the glucose concentration (glucose per 20 ounces of liquid).
5. Repeat with each liquid.

After he was done with the experiment, he put the results into the graph below.

Bar graph showing Glucose Concentration (glucose per 20 ounces of liquid) for: Chocolate Milk, Gatorade, Energy Drink, Coca Cola, Sweet Tea, Water.

1. Place the following drinks in order from least amount of glucose to most.
   - **A.** Gatorade
   - **B.** Chocolate Milk
   - **C.** Coca Cola
   - **D.** Water

   Least ⟩ ____ ⟩ ____ ⟩ ____ ⟩ ____ ⟩ Most

2. What was the main objective of Toby's experiment?
   - **A.** to show that Gatorade is healthier than soda
   - **B.** to argue against children drinking energy drinks
   - **C.** to compare the amount of glucose in drinks
   - **D.** to create an experiment with drinks

3. Which two beverages have approximately the same about of glucose?
   - **A.** Coca Cola and Energy Drink
   - **B.** Sweet Tea and Chocolate Milk
   - **C.** Water and Gatorade
   - **D.** Energy Drink and Sweet Tea

4. How did Toby determine which beverage(s) had the most amount of glucose? Give evidence from the text to support your answer.

   _____
   _____
   _____
   _____
   _____
   _____

Passage 2: A Day at Band Camp

Read the schedule, then help Judy, Jack, Ryan, and Kelly plan their day at Band Camp.

After students register, they should go to the main rehearsal room and sit with their instrument section.

Time	Activity
8:00 am	Arrival and registration
8:30 am	Group tuning and warm-up
9:15 am	Station 1- Instrument section time with the conductor
10:00 am	Station 2 - Team building
10:45 am	Station 3 - Sight-reading music practice
11:30 am	Station 4 - Rhythm games
12:15 pm	Lunch
1:30 pm	Station 5 - Try out a new instrument
2:15 pm	Station 6 - Rehearse with your instrument family
3:00 pm	Group rehearsal
4:00 pm	Final performance for family and friends

5. What should musicians do when they arrive in the morning?
    - **A.** begin warming up and practicing their music
    - **B.** register and sit with their instrument section
    - **C.** tune their instruments
    - **D.** find their friends

6. What time is the final rehearsal of the day?
    - **A.** 1:30 pm
    - **B.** 2:15 pm
    - **C.** 3:00 pm
    - **D.** 4:00 pm

7. The following question has two parts. First answer Part A. Then, answer Part B.

Part A
Ryan and his mom are stuck in traffic on the way to Band Camp. It is 8:10 am and they estimate it will take another 15 minutes to arrive. Will Ryan make it in time for the beginning of camp?
- **A.** Yes, with 5 minutes left to register.
- **B.** Yes, but without any time to register.
- **C.** No, Ryan will arrive in the middle of warm-up.
- **D.** No, Ryan will miss part of Station 1.

Part B
Which detail from the text supports the answer in Part A?
- **A.** Group tuning and warm-up lasts until 9:15 am.
- **B.** Team building occurs after Station 1.
- **C.** Station 1 begins at 9:15 am.
- **D.** Registration lasts until 8:30 am.

8. The conductor would like to meet with all trumpet players from 1:15-2:45 pm. Kelly plays trumpet. What parts of camp will she miss? Use information from the schedule to support your answer.

EXPLAIN HOW AUTHORS USE EVIDENCE TO SUPPORT POINT OF VIEW

RI.4.8 Explain how an author uses reasons and evidence to support particular points in a text.

Directions: Read the passage and answer the questions below.

Passage 1: Biomimicry

1   Have you ever wondered where inventors get their ideas? Would you be surprised to know many of them come from nature? Plants and animals adapt to their surroundings in order to survive. A kind of science called biomimicry looks at how humans can learn from nature and apply it to our own lives. Bio means "life," and mimic means "to copy." So, with biomimicry we copy the best parts of nature to solve human problems.

2   Maybe the most famous example of biomimicry is Velcro. The inventor of Velcro noticed that when his dog ran through a field, he became covered in burr seeds. These burrs were so hard to pick off that he looked at one under a microscope. He noticed that the burr had tiny hooks that would catch on fibers like his dog's hair. He invented Velcro with similar hooks and loops to attach things together.

3   Another example from nature is from thorns. The long, thorny stems of a briar patch protect the plant from predators. Humans developed barbed wire to for protection too. On a farm, barbed wire keeps livestock in, and predators out.

4   Humans mimic animal adaptations too. For example, a human problem is that biking and skateboarding are dangerous. If we look at nature, the turtle has a hard shell to protect its body from predators. So, a solution to the human problem copies turtle shells, giving us helmets. Camouflage is a similar adaptation humans adopted.

5   People are constantly inventing new things that make our life safer and easier. By looking at nature, we can see how animals and plants have already adapted. Using these ideas we can work together with nature to make our lives less challenging. So the next time you encounter a problem, think about whether the issue has already been solved… in nature!

1. What main point is the author trying to make?
    A. Animals and plants survive because they adapt to the environment.
    B. Animals are easier for humans to copy than plants.
    C. A famous inventor used biomimicry to create Velcro.
    D. Humans copy nature to make our lives better.

2. Identify one fact that the author uses to support her point that nature can give us ideas that help us stay safe.

   A. Bicycle helmets are modeled after turtle shells to protect the head from danger.
   B. Velcro is adapted from burrs, which hurt animals.
   C. Bio means "life," and mimic means "to copy."
   D. People invent new things to make our lives easier.

3. Why did the author write the passage?

   A. To explain why animals and plants are interesting for humans.
   B. To convince the reader to try inventing.
   C. To explain how many human inventions come from nature.
   D. To entertain the reader with stories about inventions.

4. What evidence could the author have added to make her argument stronger?

_____

_____

_____

_____

_____

_____

Passage 2: Dangerous Devices

1   Cell phones are one of the most recent developments in modern technology. They make life more convenient. But they can also be a threat to safety. And smart phones with access to the internet may be even more dangerous!

2   Many studies show that cell phones put drivers at risk. People who talk on the phone while driving are 4 times more likely to have an accident than if they are not using their phones while driving. That doesn't even take into account people who text while driving.

3   Researchers studied 699 drivers who were in an accident while using their phones. The main reason for the accidents may surprise you. The problem was not that people used one hand for the phone and one for driving. Instead, the accidents were caused when the drivers became distracted by the phone call. As a result, the drivers lost concentration.

4   Unfortunately, most drivers report using their cell phone often while driving. It's especially common with young drivers. Twenty percent of 18-29 year-old drivers report using their phone regularly or fairly often while driving. This is even true for people who know it's dangerous.

5   Education will be an important part of stopping this problem. We must help people see that drivers who are distracted, whether through calls or texting, are a danger to everyone on the road.

5. Why did the author write this passage?
   - **A.** To teach and convince the reader that driving while distracted by a phone is dangerous.
   - **B.** To give information about the number of accidents caused by phone use.
   - **C.** To make the reader concerned about car accidents.
   - **D.** To investigate what might happen if people don't stop using phones at the wheel.

6. Which is a main point of paragraph 4?
   - **A.** People don't understand how dangerous it is to use a cell phone while driving.
   - **B.** Most people admit to using their cell phones while driving.
   - **C.** Young drivers are especially dangerous.
   - **D.** Education is the only way to stop people from using cell phones behind the wheel of a car.

7. The following question has two parts. First answer Part A. Then, answer Part B.

Part A
What is the author's main claim?
   - **A.** Nearly everyone uses a cell phone while driving.
   - **B.** There should be worse consequences for using a cell phone while driving.
   - **C.** Driving while using a cell phone is dangerous.
   - **D.** Drivers under 30 cause more accidents.

Part B
Which detail from the text supports the answer in Part A?
- **A.** "Cell phones are one of the most recent developments in modern technology."
- **B.** "They make life more convenient."
- **C.** "We must help people see that drivers who are distracted, whether through calls or texting, are a danger to everyone on the road."
- **D.** "Twenty percent of 18-29 year-old drivers report using their phone regularly or fairly often while driving."

8. Reread paragraph 1. What claim does the author make that isn't well supported? How might the author better support that claim?

INTEGRATE INFORMATION FROM TWO TEXTS

RI.4.9 Integrate information from two texts on the same topic in order to write or speak about the subject knowledgeably.

Directions: Read the passage and answer the questions below.

Passage 1: The Choice to Sit

1   One evening a tired seamstress took a seat on her bus ride home. She worked long hours at the Montgomery Fair department store and she was tired. Before she reached her bus stop, the driver ordered her to move to the back of the bus. She refused, and was arrested. But why would someone be arrested for simply sitting on a bus?

2   The year was 1955. The woman's name was Rosa Parks. And she was, in fact, breaking a law. In that time, the front 10 seats of a bus were reserved for white riders. Mrs. Parks was African American. When she sat down, Parks sat in the 11th row. The bus driver ordered her to get up because the bus was getting crowded with white passengers. Black bus riders were supposed to give white riders their seats if the white seats ran out.

3   But Rosa Parks didn't think this was fair. She challenged the idea that people should be given special privileges just because of their skin color. But what could be done? After all, this was the law. Parks put herself in danger by disobeying the laws of the city. Could one person do enough to get these laws changed?

4   Race laws were called segregation, and they didn't just apply to buses. Whites and blacks were supposed to have separate bathrooms, water fountains, and even schools. They had to sit in separate parts of a restaurant. Almost always, the buildings and sections assigned to African Americans were worse than those used by white people. During the Civil Rights movement, African Americans challenged society's treatment of them, saying it was unfair. But, with laws like segregation, would the situation ever change?

5   Eventually, segregation became against the law. One of the major reasons for change was that people like Rosa Parks were willing to stand up against it. Sometimes, standing up began with the choice to sit.

Passage 2: The Legacy of Rosa Parks

1   When Rosa Parks refused the order to move to the back of the bus, she became the Mother of Civil Rights. Even before she took a stand, Parks thought segregation was unfair. Early in her life she wrote that she would "never accept" segregation. She wanted to "search for a way of working for freedom and first class citizenship."

2   Parks worked for years as a volunteer with the NAACP, an organization dedicated to helping African Americans seek equal rights. She was the secretary. By 1955 she was discouraged. She knew something major needed to happen for change to occur. When Parks refused to give up her seat on the bus, she knew she would be arrested. But she was fed up. "I suppose when you live this experience… getting arrested doesn't seem so bad."

3   Her arrest caused a community boycott. Members of the African American community refused to ride the bus, first for a day, then a month… eventually the boycott lasted over a year. She was fired from her job shortly after her arrest. This allowed her to help organize a car-pool system where riders and drivers were matched up. She traveled the country raising awareness.

4   Her efforts helped turn the local movement into a national one. And eventually the movement started by just one woman helped to change segregation laws. But the personal cost to her and her family was difficult. She and her husband both lost their jobs. No one in town would hire them so they had to move. She became stressed and sick. Still, she carried on for the cause of equality. Throughout her life, Rosa Parks tried to stand up for her own rights and those of her African American brothers and sisters.

1. Which question from Passage 1 is best answered by Passage 2?
    A. "But why would someone be arrested for simply sitting on a bus?"
    B. "But what could be done?"
    C. "Could one person do enough to get these laws changed?"
    D. But, with laws like segregation, would the situation ever change?

2. The column on the left lists some key ideas and information about Rosa Parks. One idea is found in both Passage 1 and Passage 2. One idea is found in Passage 1 only, and one idea is found in Passage 2 only. Place the ideas in the correct columns below. Please note that one idea does not belong in either column.

Important ideas about Rosa Parks	Both Passages	Passage 1	Passage 2
Rosa Parks organized a car-pool system that helped African Americans boycott the bus for years.			
Rosa Parks was tired after a long day's work when she decided not to move to the back of the bus.			
Rosa Parks believed that it was unfair for blacks and whites to have separate seats.			
Rosa Parks soon gave up fighting against inequality.			

3. Which detail in Passage 2 helped you understand the negative effect of Rosa Parks' actions on her personal life?
    A. She created a community boycott.
    B. She lost her job and became sick.
    C. She traveled the country.
    D. She was no longer allowed to ride the bus.

4. Given the information presented in these two texts, explain how Rosa Parks impacted the cause of equality. Give evidence from the text to support your answer.

_____

_____

_____

_____

5. Read the following paragraph and highlight the least important detail in this passage.
    Parks worked for years as a volunteer with the NAACP, an organization dedicated to helping African Americans seek equal rights. She was the secretary. By 1955 she was discouraged. She knew something major needed to happen for change to occur. When Parks refused to give up her seat on the bus, she knew she would be arrested. But she was fed up. "I suppose when you live this experience… getting arrested doesn't seem so bad."

READING: INFORMATION

6. One important detail in Passage 2 that was left out of Passage 1 is
   A. "She was fired from her job shortly after her arrest."
   B. "Even before she took a stand, Parks thought segregation was unfair."
   C. "When Parks refused to give up her seat on the bus, she knew she would be arrested."
   D. "She knew something major needed to happen for change to occur."

7. The following question has two parts. First answer Part A. Then, answer Part B.

Part A

What topic is more fully explained by Passage 1 than Passage 2?
   A. the concept of segregation
   B. the consequences on society as a result of Park's actions
   C. Park's arrest
   D. the national movement caused by the boycott

Part B

Which detail from the text supports the answer in Part A?
   A. "But Rosa Parks didn't think this was fair."
   B. "Parks put herself in danger by disobeying the laws of the city."
   C. "Whites and blacks were supposed to have separate bathrooms, water fountains, and even schools."
   D. "But, with laws like segregation, would the situation ever change?"

8. If you were to write about Rosa Parks' impact on equality, how would you decide what details were important enough to include? Is there anything in either text that the author didn't include that you think is important to write about to help the reader understand the topic?

78 READING: INFORMATION

LANGUAGE

HAVE COMMAND OF GRAMMAR & USAGE

L.4.1 Demonstrate command of the conventions of standard English grammar and usage when writing or speaking.

Use Relative Pronouns and Adverbs
L.4.1A Use relative pronouns *(who, whose, whom, which, that)* **and relative adverbs** *(where, when, why).*

1. Identify the relative pronoun in the sentence below.
   The girl who stole your bike has been caught at her school.
   - **A.** girl
   - **B.** who
   - **C.** has been
   - **D.** her

2. Which of the following sentences correctly uses a relative pronoun?
   - **A.** He couldn't play, that surprised me.
   - **B.** She is the girl whose plays basketball.
   - **C.** A teacher is someone who helps us learn.
   - **D.** Winter is the time which it gets cold.

3. Determine the correct word for the sentence below.
   The shoes _____ Josie chose for the dance are too small.
   - **A.** that
   - **B.** who
   - **C.** where
   - **D.** what

4. Read the following sentence. Then choose the correct relative pronoun or adverb to replace the underlined error.
   We have always known that Jack is someone <u>that's talents</u> would make him famous.
   - **A.** who talents
   - **B.** whose talents
   - **C.** which talents
   - **D.** who is talents

LANGUAGE

Use Progressive Verb Tenses

L.4.1B Form and use the progressive *(e.g., I was walking; I am walking; I will be walking)* verb tenses.

1. Which of the following sentences correctly shows **present** progressive tense?
    - **A.** Our robotics team would plan a trip to Disney World.
    - **B.** Our robotics team is planning a trip to Disney World.
    - **C.** Our robotics team might plan a trip to Disney World.
    - **D.** Our robotics team will be planning a trip to Disney World.

2. Which sentence does NOT use progressive tense correctly?
    - **A.** Last year, Julian is playing soccer.
    - **B.** The color guard will be performing in the Thanksgiving parade.
    - **C.** I am going to the store with my mom.
    - **D.** We are making tacos for dinner tonight.

3. Which sentence correctly revises the sentence below by using **past progressive tense**?
    When I walked to the store, I came across a shiny penny.
    - **A.** When I walked to the store, I will come across a shiny penny.
    - **B.** When I am walking to the store, I came across a shiny penny.
    - **C.** When I walked to the store, I was coming across a shiny penny.
    - **D.** When I was walking to the store, I came across a shiny penny.

4. Complete the chart with sentences that use the appropriate progressive tenses for the phrase **I swim.**

past progressive	
present progressive	
future progressive	

Use Modal Auxiliaries

L.4.1C Use modal auxiliaries *(e.g., can, may, must)* to convey various conditions.

1. Which auxiliary verb shows a past ability to do something?
    - **A.** can
    - **B.** might
    - **C.** could
    - **D.** would

LANGUAGE

2. Which of the following sentences correctly uses a modal auxiliary verb?
    A. We would see warmer days in the summer.
    B. That branch might fall at any moment.
    C. They might study to pass the test.
    D. We were tired last night.

3. Read the following sentence. Choose the correct auxiliary verb.
   You _____ tell me how to get there so I can pick you up.
    A. couldn't
    B. may
    C. must
    D. might

4. Dan's parents tell him it is his choice whether to play in the game. Which modal auxiliary verb is correct?
    A. He would play.
    B. He can play.
    C. He must play.
    D. He will play.

Order Adjectives
L.4.1D Order adjectives within sentences according to conventional patterns (e.g., a small red bag rather than a red small bag).

1. Which sentence correctly orders the adjectives?
    A. Julie put the brownies in a large glass plan.
    B. Allison washed her car with a round small sponge.
    C. Tiffany gave baby a plastic colorful rattle.
    D. Sarah's quilt has a square small hole in the bottom.

2. Place the adjectives below in their correct order.
   old / the / chair / wooden / rocking
    A. the old rocking wooden chair
    B. the old wooden rocking chair
    C. the wooden old rocking chair
    D. the old wooden chair rocking

3. Correct the sentence below by placing the adjectives in their correct order.
   The playset has brown, huge, long ropes for swinging.
    A. The playset has long, huge, brown ropes for swinging.
    B. The playset has brown, long, huge ropes for swinging.
    C. The playset has huge, long, brown ropes for swinging.
    D. The huge playset has brown long ropes for swinging.

4. Which sentence does NOT order the adjectives correctly?
   A. The warm blackberry pie is in the oven.
   B. The karate master has a black long belt.
   C. The young black cat is hungry.
   D. The yellow cotton t-shirt is in the wash.

Form & Use Prepositional Phrases
L.4.1E Form and use prepositional phrases.

1. Choose the best preposition to fill in the blank.
   The power button is _____ the computer monitor.
   A. towards
   B. across
   C. underneath
   D. between

2. Choose the correctly underlined prepositional phrase in the following sentence.
   Find the main idea of the book.
   A. <u>Find the main idea</u> of the book.
   B. Find the main idea <u>of the book.</u>
   C. Find the <u>main idea</u> of the book.
   D. Find the <u>main idea of the book.</u>

3. Choose the word that is the object of the preposition in the following sentence.
   Have you ever been to Morocco?
   A. have
   B. you
   C. Morocco
   D. to

4. Choose the best preposition(s) to fill in the blank.
   I went to the school dance _____ the other students.
   A. among
   B. with
   C. around
   D. between

5. Select the sentence with the correct prepositional phrase.
   A. Leo is cowering within the corner.
   B. Leo is cowering at the corner.
   C. Leo is cowering beside the corner.
   D. Leo is cowering in the corner.

Fragments, Run-ons and Sentences
L.4.1F Produce complete sentences, recognizing and correcting inappropriate fragments and run-ons.

1. Which sentence is a run-on sentence?
   - **A.** Put on your helmet to stay safe on your bike.
   - **B.** You need to stay safe, so put on your helmet.
   - **C.** Put on your helmet stay safe on your bike.
   - **D.** In order to stay safe, put on your helmet.

2. A student has written the following run-on sentence:
   I enjoyed the basketball game do you want to go tomorrow?
   Which of the following revisions correctly edits the run-on sentence?
   - **A.** I enjoyed the basketball game, do you want to go tomorrow?
   - **B.** I enjoyed the basketball game. Do you want to go tomorrow?
   - **C.** I enjoyed the basketball game and do you want to go tomorrow?
   - **D.** I enjoyed the basketball game, want to go tomorrow?

3. Which sentence correctly revises the run-on sentence below by adding a conjunction?
   The sun is hot, wear sunscreen.
   - **A.** The sun is hot. Wear sunscreen.
   - **B.** The sun is hot, so wear sunscreen.
   - **C.** The sun is hot and wear sunscreen.
   - **D.** The sun is hot wear sunscreen.

4. The following question has two parts. First answer Part A. Then, answer Part B.

Part A
Read the following paragraph. **Underline** the run-on sentence.
My dad needs to fix the water spout outside. He says we need to start before it gets dark, the darkness will make it hard to see. The sun is beginning to go down. I get my headlamp just in case we can't see.

Part B
Revise the run on-on sentence as a complete sentence.

_____

_____

_____

Use Frequently Confused Words

L.4.1G Correctly use frequently confused words *(e.g., to, too, two; there, their)*.

1. Choose the sentence that is correct.
   - **A.** There are two many choices!
   - **B.** There are too many choices!
   - **C.** There are to many choices!
   - **D.** The choices are to many!

2. Choose the correct answer to complete the sentence below.
   There are _____ dogs over _____.
   - **A.** too; there
   - **B.** to; their
   - **C.** two; there
   - **D.** two; their

3. Choose the sentence that is correct.
   - **A.** Their are not enough seats for everyone.
   - **B.** Santos use to live on the beach.
   - **C.** The students need to right the sentence correctly.
   - **D.** You're the best!

4. Rewrite the sentence using the correctly spelled words.
   Wear are you planning to spend you're Christmas break?

   _____

   _____

   _____

KNOW CAPITALIZATION, PUNCTUATION & SPELLING

L.4.2 Demonstrate command of the conventions of standard English capitalization, punctuation, and spelling when writing.

Use Correct Capitalization
L.4.2A Use correct capitalization.

1. Identify the sentence with correct capitalization.
   - **A.** Joe purchased Potato Soup from a restaurant called Soups & more in Arlington, Virginia.
   - **B.** Joe purchased potato soup from a Restaurant called Soups & More in Arlington, Virginia.
   - **C.** Joe purchased potato soup from a restaurant called Soups & More in Arlington, Virginia.
   - **D.** Joe purchased potato soup from a restaurant called soups & more in Arlington, virginia.

2. Which of the following sentences has an error in capitalzation?
   - **A.** I told Sally how to get to the grocery story on the corner of Main Street and 4th Street.
   - **B.** Do you want to meet me at the park to play basketball?
   - **C.** I have attended Bakersville Elementary school in Mrs. helgesen's class.
   - **D.** Would anyone like to go fishing in the Columbia River?

3. Which word in the following sentence should be capitalized?
   We got to the corner ticket office before dawn to buy concert tickets for sarah and her friends.
   - **A.** Corner
   - **B.** Office
   - **C.** Dawn
   - **D.** Sarah

4. Rewrite the following sentence with correct capitalization.
   Do you and joshua remember the name of the store where we bought kansas city souvenirs?

   _____

   _____

   _____

86   LANGUAGE

Use Commas and Quotation Marks in Direct Speech
L.4.2B Use commas and quotation marks to mark direct speech and quotations from a text.

1. Choose the sentence that has the correct punctuation.
   - **A.** "I answered the phone," and said I think you have the wrong number."
   - **B.** I answered the phone and said, "I think you have the wrong number."
   - **C.** "I answered the phone" and said, "I think you have the wrong number."
   - **D.** I answered the phone and said, "that I think you have the wrong number."

2. Read the following paragraph and determine which sentence has the incorrect punctuation of direct speech.

   1 **I got to the soccer field late, because I missed my bus.** 2 **"Please stretch out," my coach said.** 3 **"I already did, I told him."** 4 **My coach responded, "Alright, get on the field!"**
   - **A.** Sentence 1
   - **B.** Sentence 2
   - **C.** Sentence 3
   - **D.** Sentence 4

3. Where in the following sentence would you place a comma?

   "I was wondering" she said "what did you bring for lunch today?"
   - **A.** after the word 'wondering' and after the word 'what'
   - **B.** after the word 'said' and after the word 'you'
   - **C.** after the word 'wondering' and after the word 'said'
   - **D.** after the word 'said' and after the word 'today'

4. Rewrite the following sentence with correct quotation marks and punctuation.

   Wow! What a great experience, said Dan. I know I'll come back.

   _____

   _____

Use Commas and Coordinating Conjunctions
L.4.2C Use a comma before a coordinating conjunction in a compound sentence.

1. Which sentence has the correct punctuation?
   - **A.** We all ran downstairs, and Bobby lunged for the door.
   - **B.** The boys stood around talking, and teasing one another.
   - **C.** The family was eating dinner last night when, they heard a knock at the door.
   - **D.** We looked at one another and, June burst into laughter.

2. How should the following sentence be punctuated?
   A huge gust of wind shook the trees and the bird's egg fell from the nest.
   - A. A comma belongs after the word "shook."
   - B. A comma belongs after the word "trees."
   - C. A comma belongs after the word "and."
   - D. This sentence does not need a comma.

3. Read the following sentence, then fill in the chart.

Independent Clause #1	Independent Clause #2	Coordinating Conjunction	Comma Placement
I'm practicing math every night	I can win the mathlete competition		

4. Rewrite the following sentences as a single compound sentence with a coordinating conjunction and comma in the correct place.
   Charlie likes to listen to music on Pandora. Cerise prefers to play games on a tablet.

   _____

   _____

   _____

Spell Correctly
L.4.2.D Spell grade-appropriate words correctly, consulting references as needed.

1. Which word in the sentence below is spelled incorrectly?
   The entertaining teacher emphesized his point and repeated the instructions loudly.
   - A. entertaining
   - B. emphesized
   - C. repeated
   - D. instructions

2. Which word in the list below is spelled correctly?
   - A. problum
   - B. cumpas
   - C. axcept
   - D. catch

3. Choose the correct spelling of the underlined word.

   The <u>villain</u> in the movie committed many evil deeds.

       A. villan
       B. villin
       C. villen
       D. the word is correct as written

4. Fill in the chart with the correct number of syllables for each spelling word.

Word	Syllables
vocal	
proposal	
twelve	
inverse	
canopy	

USE APPROPRIATE LANGUAGE CONVENTIONS TO CONVEY IDEAS

L.4.3 Use knowledge of language and its conventions when writing, speaking, reading, or listening.

Choose Words & Phrases to Convey Ideas
L.4.3A Choose words and phrases to convey ideas precisely.

1. Read the sentence below. Then choose a more precise and descriptive word to replace the underlined word in the sentence.
   The boy <u>crawled</u> along the floor, desperate not to be seen.
   - **A.** sat
   - **B.** slithered
   - **C.** slowed
   - **D.** moved

2. Place the following adjectives meaning "wet" in order from least intense to most intense: **soggy, drenched, moist.**

   Least 1. _____ 2. _____ 3. _____ Most Intense

3. There are many synonyms for the word "smart." Choose the best replacement adjective for the word "smart" in the sentence below.
   Listen to the advice of your elders, for they have many experiences which make them <u>smart</u>.
   - **A.** alert
   - **B.** nimble
   - **C.** crafty
   - **D.** wise

4. Explain the difference between "intelligent," and "crafty," which are two synonyms of the word 'smart'.

   _____
   _____
   _____

LANGUAGE

Choose Punctuation for Effect.
L.4.3B Choose Punctuation for Effect

1. Read the sentence carefully. Determine if it is a statement, a question, a command, or an exclamation. Then choose the appropriate ending punctuation.
   Oh dear, my favorite shirt is completely ruined _____
   - **A.** statement (.)
   - **B.** question (?)
   - **C.** exclamation (!)
   - **D.** command (!)

2. Read the sentence carefully. Determine if it is a statement, a question, a command, or an exclamation. Then choose the appropriate ending punctuation.
   Everyone in the class is ready to walk down the hall _____
   - **A.** statement (.)
   - **B.** question (?)
   - **C.** exclamation (!)
   - **D.** command (!)

3. Which answer choice shows the correct use of quotation marks?
   - **A.** "How in the world did you do that?" she asked.
   - **B.** "Will you come to my house tonight exclaimed Anthony?"
   - **C.** Joseph said "Wait, I want dinner too"!
   - **D.** Should we all play outside for a bit? "the mother asked."

4. Rewrite the following sentence using a dash or comma to separate the interjection from the rest of the sentence. Then add the appropriate ending punctuation.
   "Oh no what am I going to do about this science project"

   _____

   _____

   _____

   _____

Differentiate Contexts for Formal English & Informal Discourse

L.4.3C Differentiate between contexts that call for formal English (e.g., presenting ideas) and situations where informal discourse is appropriate (e.g., small-group discussion).

1. Select the sentence that is an example of informal English.
    - **A.** My presentation today will teach you about various types of sea life.
    - **B.** Good morning scholars, my name is Mr. Smith and I will be your teacher.
    - **C.** Last summer I met a young woman who was interested in furthering her education.
    - **D.** Something tells me it's gonna be a fun day.

2. Select the sentence that is an example of formal English.
    - **A.** Hey, what's up?
    - **B.** Bro, what are you up to today?
    - **C.** Would you like for me to reevaluate your status?
    - **D.** Did you see that wicked trick I did on the slide?

3. In the chart below, change the informal words or phrases to formal language using the word bank provided.

Word Bank:
nevertheless
contact
How are you?
Just wanted to let you know…
explode
Are you okay?

Informal	Formal
What's up?	
anyways	
blow up	

LANGUAGE

4. Write a persuasive letter to your principal explaining why every student should have access to an iPad. Use formal language and give three reasons to support your opinion.

_____ (Date)

_____ (Principal Name)

_____ (School Name)

_____ (Address)

_____ (City, State, Zip Code)

Dear _____ (Principal Name),

_____

_____

_____

_____

_____

_____

_____

_____

_____

_____

Sincerely,

_____ (Name)

DETERMINE MEANING OF UNKNOWN WORDS WHEN READING

L.4.4 Determine or clarify the meaning of unknown and multiple-meaning words and phrases based on grade 4 reading and content, choosing flexibly from a range of strategies.

Use Context Clues To Determine Word Meaning
L.4.4A Use context (e.g., definitions, examples, or restatements in text) as a clue to the meaning of a word or phrase.

Read the passage from the story "Ali Baba and the Forty Thieves" and answer the following questions.

1   There once lived in a town of Persia two brothers, one named Cassim, and the other Ali Baba. Their father divided a small inheritance equally between them. Cassim married a very rich wife, and became a **wealthy** merchant. Ali Baba married a woman as poor as himself, and lived by cutting wood, and bringing it upon three donkeys into the town to sell.

2   One day, when Ali Baba was in the forest, and had just cut wood enough to load his donkeys, he saw at a distance a great cloud of dust, which seemed to approach him. He observed it with attention, and **distinguished** soon after a body of horsemen, whom he suspected might be robbers. He determined to leave his donkeys to save himself. He climbed up a large tree, planted on a high rock, whose branches were thick enough to conceal him, and yet enabled him to see all that passed without being discovered.

3   The troop, who were to the number of forty, all well mounted and armed, came to the foot of the rock on which the tree stood, and there dismounted. Every man unbridled his horse, tied him to some shrub, and hung about his neck a bag of corn. Then each of them took off his saddle-bag, which seemed to Ali Baba to be full of gold and silver from its weight. One, whom he took to be their captain, came under the tree in which Ali Baba was concealed; and, making his way through some shrubs, pronounced these words—"Open, Sesame!" As soon as the captain of the robbers had thus spoken, a door opened in the rock; and after he had made all his troop enter before him, he followed them, when the door shut again of itself.

4   The robbers stayed some time within the rock, during which Ali Baba, fearful of being caught, remained in the tree.

5   At last the door opened again, and as the captain went in last, so he came out first, and stood to see them all pass by him; when Ali Baba heard him make the door close by pronouncing these words, "Shut, Sesame!" Every man at once went and bridled his horse, fastened his wallet, and mounted again. When the captain saw them all ready, he put himself at their head, and they returned the way they had come.

6   Ali Baba followed them with his eyes as far as he could see them, and afterward stayed a considerable time before he descended. Remembering the words the captain of the robbers used to cause the door to open and shut, he had the curiosity to try if his pronouncing them would have the same effect. Accordingly, he went among the shrubs, and perceiving the door concealed behind them, stood before it and said, "Open, Sesame!" The door instantly flew wide open.

7   Ali Baba, who expected a dark, dismal cavern, was surprised to see a well-lighted and spacious chamber, which received the light from an opening at the top of the rock, and in which were all sorts of provisions, rich bales of silk, stuff, brocade[1], and valuable carpeting, piled upon one another, gold and silver ingots[2] in great heaps, and money in bags. The sight of all these riches made him suppose that this cave must have been occupied for ages by robbers, who had succeeded one another.

[1] rich, silk woven fabric
[2] metal bars

1. This question has two parts. First, answer Part A. Then, answer part B.

Part A
What is the meaning of the word *wealthy* as it is used in paragraph 1?
- **A.** slow
- **B.** poor
- **C.** rich
- **D.** winning

Part B
Which detail from the passage supports the answer to Part A?
- **A.** "married a very rich wife"
- **B.** "married a woman as poor as himself"
- **C.** "lived by cutting wood"
- **D.** "divided a small inheritance"

2. Which context clue supports the meaning for the word *distinguished* (paragraph 2) as "saw"?
- **A.** "suspected might be robbers"
- **B.** "determined to save"
- **C.** "observed it with attention"
- **D.** "climbed up a large tree"

LANGUAGE

3. Reread the excerpt and underline the context clues for the word *provisions*.

   Ali Baba, who expected a dark, dismal cavern, was surprised to see a well-lighted and spacious chamber, which received the light from an opening at the top of the rock, and in which were all sorts of provisions, rich bales of silk, stuff, brocade, and valuable carpeting, piled upon one another, gold and silver ingots in great heaps, and money in bags. The sight of all these riches made him suppose that this cave must have been occupied for ages by robbers, who had succeeded one another.

4. Complete the graphic organizer for the word provisions by explaining the definition and using the word in a sentence of your own.

My Definition	My Sentence

Use Greek & Latin Affixes/Roots as Clues to Word Meaning
L.4.4B Use common, grade-appropriate Greek and Latin affixes and roots as clues to the meaning of a word (e.g., *telegraph, photograph, autograph*).

1. Read the following sentence from "Ali Baba and the Forty Thieves."

   The troop, who were to the number of forty, all well mounted and armed, came to the foot of the rock on which the tree stood, and there dismounted.

   The prefix "dis-" means "apart." In this sentence the prefix "dis-" is added to the word "mounted" which changes the meaning of "mounted." Which definition fits the word "dismounted?"

   A. climbed on
   B. climbed off
   C. stood before
   D. stood behind

2. Write a word using each prefix in the chart below. Then write a definition of the word you chose based on the prefix and root.

Prefix	Meaning	My Word
mis-	wrongly	1.
inter-	between	2.
pre-	before	3.
re-	again	4.

96 LANGUAGE

Word Definitions:

Definiition of Word 1 _____

_____

Definiition of Word 2 _____

_____

Definiition of Word 3 _____

_____

Definiition of Word 4 _____

_____

3. Read the sentence below. Then identify the meaning of the suffix -ation.

   In John's determination to get the capitalization right on his spelling test, he practiced every night, earning a reputation of a good student.

   The suffix -ation means:
   A. before
   B. relating to
   C. able to
   D. action

4. Read the following excerpt from the book "Ali Baba and the Forty Thieves."

   She ran to Ali Baba in great alarm, and said: "I believe, brother-in-law, that you know Cassim is gone to the forest, and upon what account; it is now night, and he has not returned; I am afraid some misfortune has happened to him."

   How would the meaning of the excerpt change if the text said: "...I am afraid some fortune has happened to him..."?

   _____

   _____

   _____

LANGUAGE

Know How To Use Reference Materials To Clarify Word Meaning

L.4.4C Consult reference materials (e.g., dictionaries, glossaries, thesauruses), both print and digital, to find the pronunciation and determine or clarify the precise meaning of key words and phrases.

1. Reread this sentence from "Ali Baba and the Forty Thieves." Then read the dictionary entry and complete the question.

   "Their father divided a small inheritance equally between them."

   in•her•it•ance [in-**her**-i-*tuh* ns]
   noun

   1. something that is or will be inherited (given, often after death)
   2. often money or another material possession passed from parent to child or grandchild
   3. genetic characteristics passed from parent to child

   Which sentence uses the meaning of the word *inheritance* as it is used in the excerpt from "Ali Baba and the Forty Thieves?" Circle **ALL** that apply.

   Inheritance is most often used as a noun.

   The children's inheritance of brown eyes were their favorite feature.

   The grandchildren's inheritance means that they can afford college.

2. Read the excerpt from "Ali Baba and the Forty Thieves."
   "Ali Baba, who expected a dark, dismal cavern, was surprised to see a well-lighted and spacious chamber..."

   Now read the dictionary entry and complete the task that follows.

   spa•cious [**spey**-sh*uh* s]
   adjective

   From the Latin word for space and the suffix -ous, meaning "full of".
   1. containing much space
   2. having a large area

   Which choice correctly identifies the pronunciation for the word *spacious*?
       A. A Latin word meaning "space"
       B. [spey-sh*uh* s]
       C. adjective
       D. spa•cious

3. Read the sentence. Then complete the chart by using a dictionary to determine how the word 'conceal' is pronounced, which part of speech it is, and its meaning/definition.

He climbed up a large tree, planted on a high rock, whose branches were thick enough to conceal him, and yet enabled him to see all that passed without being discovered.

Word:	conceal
Pronunciation	
Part of Speech	
Meaning/ Definition	

4. Read the three dictionary definitions for the word due. Then choose the sentence that uses it as an **adjective**.

due [doo]
adjective

1. expected to arrive at a certain time
2. required or owed

noun
3. a fee or required payment

adverb
4. referring to a compass, exactly or directly

   A. I have to pay my choir dues before the first concert.
   B. They are due to arrive at 5:00 pm.
   C. We are facing due north.
   D. Will everyone please submit their dues for basketball league?

LANGUAGE

UNDERSTAND FIGURATIVE LANGUAGE

L.4.5 Demonstrate understanding of figurative language, word relationships, and nuances in word meanings.

Understand Similes and Metaphors
L.4.5A Explain the meaning of simple similes and metaphors *(e.g., as pretty as a picture)* in context.

1. Read the following sentence and identify the simile.
   The boy's boots were as muddy as pig's hooves as he trudged onto his mother's clean kitchen floor.
   - **A.** The boy's boots
   - **B.** as muddy as pig's hooves
   - **C.** as he trudged
   - **D.** his mother's clean kitchen floor

2. Read the following sentence, then determine the meaning of the underlined metaphor.
   The wave crashed into the shore, <u>a crumbling wall of water</u> that crushed the spectators.
   - **A.** the wave was as tall and destructive as a wall that crumbled into concrete
   - **B.** the wave was higher than the houses on the beach
   - **C.** the spectators on the shore did the wave
   - **D.** the wave was a surprise to the spectators on the beach, who thought it was actually a brick wall.

3. Read the following sentence.
   "That's how I feel too, Frosty," muttered the boy sadly as he saw the inflatable snowman laying flat as a pancake on his front lawn.
   Why does the author use the phrase "flat as a pancake" in the sentence?
   - **A.** The author helps the reader understand how the inflatable snowman became flat.
   - **B.** The author helps the reader understand what an inflated snowman looks like.
   - **C.** The author helps the reader understand why the boy is sad.
   - **D.** The author compares the boy's feelings to a deflated snowman to emphasize his sadness.

4. Rewrite the following sentence with a simile or metaphor.
   The girl's eyes are blue like her mother's eyes.

   _____

   _____

Understand Common Idioms, Adages, & Proverbs

L.4.5B Recognize and explain the meaning of common idioms, adages, and proverbs.

1. Read the sentence. Then identify the correct meaning of the idiom 'having second thoughts'.

    "Are you having second thoughts about entering the contest?"
    - **A.** going to think for a long period of time
    - **B.** having doubts
    - **C.** showing your thinking
    - **D.** explaining your reasons

2. Choose the correct word to complete the adage below.

    You can't teach an old _____ new tricks.
    - **A.** dog
    - **B.** cat
    - **C.** man
    - **D.** wizard

3. Choose the correct word to complete the adage below.

    _____ of a feather flock together.
    - **A.** Chickens
    - **B.** Eagles
    - **C.** Birds
    - **D.** Penguins

4. Read the following passage, then explain the meaning of the underlined adage.

    Julian spent all of his birthday money on candy and silly toys from the dollar store, while his twin brother Carl deposited his birthday money into his savings account. "You know, Julian," Carl lectured, "<u>a penny saved is a penny earned</u>."

    _____
    _____
    _____
    _____

Know Synonyms and Antonyms

L.4.5C Demonstrate understanding of words by relating them to their opposites (antonyms) and to words with similar but not identical meanings (synonyms).

1. Read the following passage from "The Story of Aladdin and His Magical Lamp."

   His son, who was called Aladdin, was a very careless and idle fellow. He was disobedient to his father and mother, and would go out early in the morning and stay out all day, playing in the streets and public places with idle children of his own age.

   What is an antonym of the word 'disobedient' as it is used in this passage?
   - A. naughty
   - B. respectful
   - C. reluctant
   - D. disgusted

2. This question has 2 parts. First, answer Part A. Then, answer part B.

Part A

Read the following passage.

Joey was disappointed by the atrocious grade on his spelling test. However, he wasn't surprised. He didn't study all week. Instead of studying, Joey played video games.

Which detail from the passage helps the reader understand the meaning of 'atrocious' as it is used in the passage?
- A. "disappointed"
- B. "spelling test"
- C. "wasn't surprised"
- D. "played video games"

Part B

Which word has the opposite meaning of atrocious?
- A. bad
- B. excellent
- C. attributed
- D. fortunate

3. Read the following sentence.

"The child was <u>happy</u> as he unwrapped Christmas gifts."

Which of the following choices is NOT an appropriate synonym for the word happy?

    A. delighted
    B. content
    C. indifferent
    D. thrilled

4. Complete the graphic below. On the left, write words that can be used as synonyms of *small*. On the right, write words that can be used as antonyms of *small*.

Synonyms of Small	Antonyms of Small
1. _____	1. _____
2. _____	2. _____
3. _____	3. _____
4. _____	4. _____

LANGUAGE   103

KNOW & USE GENERAL ACADEMIC/DOMAIN-SPECIFIC WORDS

L.4.6 Acquire and use accurately grade-appropriate general academic and domain-specific words and phrases, including those that signal precise actions, emotions, or states of being (e.g., quizzed, whined, stammered) and that are basic to a particular topic (e.g., *wildlife, conservation,* and *endangered* when discussing animal preservation).

Passage 1: Ecosystems

Directions: Read the passage and answer the questions below.

1   An ecosystem is a biological community and its environment. The way that living things interact with non-living things in the environment is very important to the ecosystem. Living things include plants, animals, insects, and tiny organisms called microorganisms. The ecosystem also has non-living things like the sun, earth, soil, weather, and atmosphere.

2   An ecosystem is in balance when everything works together as it should. When the ecosystem is in balance the living and non-living things exist in harmony. But when something disturbs the balance, it's called an intruder. Intruders can include human beings, pollution, changes in migration patterns, or the introduction of outside living things. When the stability of an ecosystem is interrupted, the ecosystem can be damaged or destroyed.

1. What does the word 'harmony' mean in the context of this passage?
    A. musical
    B. stability
    C. discord
    D. living

2. Which statement from the passage **best** supports the meaning of the word 'balance'?
   A. "everything works together"
   B. "non-living things like the sun, earth, soil"
   C. "the introduction of outside living things"
   D. "damaged or destroyed"

3. Reread this sentence.

   The way that living things interact with non-living things in the environment is very important to the ecosystem.

   The word **interact** can be replaced with the word:
   A. interfere
   B. subject
   C. cooperate
   D. understand

4. Write a definition for the word 'stability' as it is used to refer to an ecosystem.

   _____
   _____
   _____
   _____

Passage 2: Julie's Sick Day

1   When Julie got up for school, she could tell it wasn't going to be a good day. Her stomach ached and her head pounded. But she was really looking forward to her first basketball practice after school. "Do you feel alright," her mother asked at the breakfast table? "You look pale."

2   "No, I'm ok," she said, shrugging away from her mother who was trying to feel her forehead. "Really mom, I'm fine," she _____ her mom. "I'll be late for school if I don't hurry, so I'll grab breakfast at school," she called out the door.

3   But at school Julie forgot all about breakfast. She didn't have much of an appetite and felt hot and clammy. Paying attention in class was a chore—she found it harder and harder to _____. But Julie knew if she visited the nurse she would miss practice for sure.

4   Julie thought if she could just make it to recess, she could rest. But just as she walked outside, she got sick on the playground! Julie couldn't remember the last time she had been more mortified. As her teacher walked over to help, Julie hung her head in _____. The teacher tried to comfort her, but what Julie really wanted was to crawl into her own bed. As Julie headed home, she knew she probably should have stayed in bed all along.

5. Which word best replaces the blank line in paragraph 2?
    - **A.** flushed
    - **B.** yelled at
    - **C.** assured
    - **D.** exclaimed

6. Which word best replaces the blank line in paragraph 3?
    - **A.** concentrate
    - **B.** eat
    - **C.** sit
    - **D.** explain

7. Which word **best** replaces the blank line in paragraph 8?
    - **A.** envy
    - **B.** embarrassment
    - **C.** excitement
    - **D.** honor

8. Reread this sentence from paragraph 1.

   Her stomach ached and her head pounded.

   What is the effect of the author's use of the word 'pounded'?
   - A. It shows that Julie hit her head in order to try to feel better.
   - B. It emphasizes how severe Julie's headache is.
   - C. It reveals that Julie has a headache from the pounding basketball.
   - D. It shows that Julie isn't really sick at all.

Passage 3: The Scientific Method

Galileo is the scientist best known for discovering that the earth and other planets revolve around the sun. In his time, understanding the world was explained by thinkers and philosophers. But Galileo wanted to investigate those theories by doing experiments. As he studied more and more about the world around him, he wanted to test the principles he discovered to see if he could apply them in everyday life. From this basis, other scientists developed what has become the scientific method.

9. Which word **best** replaces the word 'investigate' in the passage?
   - A. publish
   - B. promote
   - C. believe
   - D. research

10. Read this sentence from the passage.

    As he studied more and more about the world around him, he wanted to test the principles he discovered to see if he could apply them in everyday life.

    What does the word 'principles' mean as it is used in this sentence? Complete the chart to define the word, then provide two context clues that support your reasoning.

Word:	Definition:
Context Clue 1	
Context Clue 2	

ANSWER EXPLANATIONS

READING: LITERATURE
RL.4.1 Understand Text: Refer to Details and Draw Inferences

1. C. The correct answer is C since the greatest danger for John is living with a dragon that wants to eat him and the townspeople. Although living in an old, abandoned castle or being in a stairwell without light could be potentially dangerous, these dangers do not pose as great a threat as living with a dragon that wants to eat humans. John could get into trouble for not paying rent for his rooms, but, again, this does not pose the greatest danger.

2. D. This is the correct answer since the best reason for John not paying rent is that the castle is abandoned and, thus "no one asked any rent". Answer choices B and C are not good reasons for not paying rent as many people provide useful services to the community, or live in small rooms, and still have to pay rent.

3. B. Magnificence is the correct synonym for splendour.

4. Part A- A The most convincing reason that the dragon wants to be found is because he wants someone to help him fix his wing. the dragon states this cleary when it says." "I'm glad you finally found me, as I should like you to do a job for me." **Part B- D.** This is the best evidence. Answer choices A and B only describe the noises the dragon is making. They don't state why the dragon is making a noise. C is irrelevant.

5. B. An isle is another word for island. The surrounding information (such as the reference to the island's place in the sea and how people can see water when they look out from the land) leads the reader to the conclusion that isle means island.

6. C. The author cherishes (loves) the country. The author proclaims that her country feels warm, green, and loving.

7. A. The author is describing what the Irish love about their country, so you can infer that they believe it is beautiful.

8. B. Only one country, Ireland, is directly referenced in the text.

9. B. The text states that dogs bury their toys due to their natural instincts. Therefore, you can infer that their instincts still drive their actions today.

10. A. You can infer that Jerome is late to soccer practice because he looks at his watch and says "oh no!", and because his coach says sarcastically "Nice of you to join us!". It is possible for Jerome to also be unorganized, but the text did not lead you to believe that he couldn't find his cleats, just that he was rushing to practice.

11. [Suggested answer: Jasmine is looking for an extra pencil because she wants to help her friend Allison. She sees that Allison has a difficult life and forgets her school materials often because she needs to take care of her younger siblings.]

RL.4.2 Determine Theme & Summarize Text

1. B. Lines 3-4 say, "One had a mouse, the other had none, And that's the way the quarrel begun."

2. Part A-A. The kittens learn it's better to get along than to fight. When the kittens were fighting, the old lady put them outside in cold weather. When they stopped fighting and calmed down, the kittens were allowed back inside.
Part B-D. These lines show that the kittens learned that things got better when they calmed down and got along rather than when they quarreled.

3. Example answer: The old woman was cleaning the room and needed the fighting kittens out of the way, and wanted the kittens to stop fighting.

4. Example answer: The poem is about two kittens who learn that it is better to get along than to fight. The poem takes place on a stormy winter night (lines 1 and 9 both tell that it was a stormy night). At first, the kittens are fighting over a mouse, and so the old lady puts them outside into the stormy night, where "the ground is covered in frost and snow (line 13)", so she can sweep the floor. The kittens decide to stop fighting because they are outside in a storm and have "nowhere to go" (line 14). The author shows that they were uncomfortable outside as they were "all wet with the snow," and, "cold as ice" (line 18) when they eventually were let back in. This shows how the setting, a cold winter night, contributes to the kitten realising that fighting is not a good idea as they have to sit in the cold as a punishment. When they calm down, the kittens are allowed back inside into the house, and they have learned their lesson that it is better to get along than to fight, so you can be in the warm house.

5. A. The author uses her father's knowledge of the jungle to help her survive. Her father taught her to follow water if she ever got lost in the jungle, so she walks beside a stream until she comes to the hut. Her father also taught her that much of the food in the jungle is poisonous, so she just drinks lots of water.

6. B. One theme of this passage is that key skills and knowledge can aid survival in the wild. Airplane crashes are frightening, but this is not the main theme of the passage. The crash is only mentioned at the beginning of the passage.

7. A. Paragraph 4 shows that the author found the hut just in time. She was desperately hungry and could barely walk. Though she survived as long as she did because of the things her father had taught her, she probably couldn't have survived much longer if she hadn't wandered into the hut and met the men who fed her and reunited her with her father.

8. Example answer: The author's knowledge of the jungle, which she had learned from her father, helped her survive. For example, she followed the stream in the jungle and she did not eat anything from the land in case it might be poisonous, as her father had told her. She also found a bag of candy that someone had on the plane, which gave her at least some energy to go on. It was the only food she ate during the 10 days she was in the jungle. She also found a hut, which gave her a place to shelter when she was very weak, and was the place where the men who helped save her found her.

RL.4.3 Describe Character, Setting and Events

1. C. The queen wants to determine if the young woman is truly a princess like she says. The other answer choices are unsupported by the text.

2. B. This detail from the story shows that the princess is truly a princess. The other details do not support that claim.

3. A. The word "satisfied" describes the prince because he has finally found a true princess to marry. The other word choices are not supported by details from the text.

4. Example answer: The description of the night, "a terrible storm," and the young woman's physical condition, "The water ran down from her hair and clothes," make the reader wonder whether this woman can really be a princess, which builds suspense about whether she will detect the pea under the mattress or not.

5. Example answer:

Phrase that Describes the Setting	Evidence From "The Ants & the Grasshopper"
a warm Autumn day	bright day in late autumn
	bustling about in the warm sunshine

6. B. The word "humbly" allows the reader to know that the grasshopper is sheepishly asking the ants for food, embarrassed that he doesn't have any. The word "humbly" comes before the word "begged", which indicates that the grasshopper hopes to get something from the ants and therefore would probably not act 'angry and demanding'.

Asking in a "generous" way does not make sense in this context. The grasshopper is starving so he would not feel "happy and full".

7. Part A- C. The reader can infer that the ants believe the grasshopper was foolish by the way they respond to him, ultimately ignoring him after making fun of him.

Part B- B. This detail shows that the ants feel the grasshopper was foolish. The word "disgust" reveals the feelings of the ants towards the grasshopper. None of the other answer choices show details how the ants feel toward the grasshopper.

8. Example answer: It reveals that the ants are not sympathetic to the grasshopper's needs because they feel that he should have spent his time in the summer collecting food rather than playing music. It then says that they turn their back on him and continue their work, supporting the claim that they do not feel sorry for him or feel like they owe him food.

RL.4.4 Determine Word Meaning in Text

1. C. The word "mounted" refers to Jessie getting onto her unicycle. Therefore the correct meaning is "climbed on."

2. A. "Catastrophe" can best be replaced with the word "disaster." At this point in the story things are not going right for Jessie.

3. B. The word "teetering" means that the ball is hovering between going into the basket or not. It adds suspense because the reader doesn't know whether it will go in or not.

4. Example answer: The word "sailed" makes the reader think that the shots are coming easily. This is supported by the statement in the text that "Jessie relaxed her body" and that she'd done this "a hundred times before."

5. B. This phrase indicates that Jessie is nervous. The other answer choices are not supported by the text.

6.

Definition:	serious or harsh	
	Evidence from the text	Explanation of how text evidence supports the definition
#1	"He towered over Jessie, unsmiling, and examined his clipboard…"	This shows the man's serious nature. The fact that he isn't smiling and is examining the clipboard show he is serious and all business.
#2	"He frowned as he inspected…"	The man's frown is because he is very serious about the job he is doing, and has no thought of anything fun or lighthearted.

7. Part A- A. The term "Achilles heel" refers to

a person's weak or vulnerable spot or area. It is derived from the Greek myth of Achilles and his mother Thetis.

Part B- B. The phrase "her downfall" helps the reader understand the meaning of Achilles heel.

8. Example answer: Having the Midas Touch means that a person is very lucky or has the ability to be successful, like King Midas, who turned everything he touched to gold. This helps the reader understand that Jessie is successful in her quest to achieve the world record she sought, and helps the reader understand the significance of Jessie's accomplishment.

RL.4.5 Explain Structural Differences between Poems, Drama and Pros

1. C. The text is in prose structure, with paragraphs and dialogue. The other answer choices are incorrect.

2. D. There is no dialogue in the poem. However, it does include rhyme, rhythm, and stanzas.

3. A. Passage 1 is organized by paragraphs. Stage directions are for dramas, while verses are another word for stanzas, usually used in poetry. Writing is not specific enough to be a correct answer.

4. Sample answer: A drama has characters, dialogue, stage directions, and a stage setting. It is usually organized into acts and/or scenes. The characters are usually listed at the beginning of the play in the order that they appear. The stage setting tells the reader or viewers where and when the play takes place. The dialogue, or lines that the characters say to one another, are the major way the audience knows what is happening. Stage directions appear in parentheses in the play and tell the characters how to act.

5. A. This dialogue helps the reader know what is happening in the plot. It does not give a consistent rhythmic flow or pattern (which would be more related to poetry) nor does it give background knowledge.

6. B. The stage directions tell the reader who is present (the pirate crew), where they are, and what they are doing. This tells the reader the setting, not the solution, character descriptions, or who is speaking.

7. Part A- B. Both the poem and story include dialogue. Only the poem includes rhythm and rhyme. Neither includes stage directions.

Part B- B. The poem addresses Nag. The other answer choices are incorrect.

8.

"Rikki Tikki Tavi"	Structural Elements	Text Evidence	Explanation
Literary Format: prose	1. paragraphs 2. dialogue	1. "This is the story of the great war that Rikki-tikki-tavi fought single-handed…" 2. "No," said his mother; "let's take him in and dry him. he isn't really dead."	1. paragraphs organize the information 2. dialogue shows the exact words spoken by characters

"Dust of Snow"	Structural Elements	Text Evidence	Explanation
Literary Format: poem	1. rhyme 2. stanzas	1. "crow/ snow" 2. Has given my heart A change of mood And saved some part Of a day I had rued.	1. rhyme adds literary interest and contributes to rhythm 2. stanzas organize the poem into ideas

RL.4.6 Compare and Contrast Point of View

1. C. The passage is told in third-person point of view by an outside narrator.

2. C. The passage is mostly told in third-person point of view by an outside narrator.

3. Part A- A. In paragraph 2 the narrator slips into second-person for a brief moment with the line addressed directly to the reader, "You can probably guess what happened next." **Part B- B.**

4. C. The speaker in both passages is an outside observer. The narrator describes all of the elements of the story, including what the characters think, say, and do.

5. Example answer: The author believes that Icarus was too child-like to follow his father's directions. He becomes too excited to fly and forgets his father's lectures of safety. The author's point of view supports the theme that there are risks to freedom, especially for a young and inexperienced person, and also the point of view that a young person/child should listen to their parents.

6.

"The Wonderful Wizard of Oz"	"The Myth of Icarus and Daedelus"
"She thought this was very kind and thoughtful of the Scarecrow…"	"He wanted to use the wings to escape."
"But the Scarecrow did not mind how long it took him to fill the basket…"	"He was filled with sadness."

7. D. The narrator's description of Icarus tells the reader that Icarus is young and somewhat foolish. He is so excited about flying that he doesn't listen to his father's instructions and it costs him his life.

8. Example answer: The passage is written in

the third person, and tells the thoughts and feelings of more than one character (Dorothy and the Scarecrow). If it was written in first-person narration, the reader would probably not understand as much about all the feelings and thoughts of the characters in the story as it would be told from only one perspective.

9. Example answer: I was imprisoned with my son, Icarus, by an evil man on an island. We were surrounded by high walls, and the island was surrounded by water. One day, I came up with the idea to make wings from bird feathers and wax to escape. However, I told my son not to fly too close to the sun when we escaped - otherwise the wings made of wax would melt. Sadly, my son Icarus was too excited about flying and he did not listen to my instructions. He flew too close to the hot sun. The wax melted, and he fell into the sea. I only saw the feathers floating on the water, and knew that my son had drowned. I was filled with sadness. In my son's honor, I named the nearest island Icaria.

RL.4.7 Use Images to Understand Text

1. Part A- B. The illustration shows the tiger pouncing on the Mouse Deer. The other answer choices are incorrect.

Part B- A. The best support is in the text where the Tiger speaks to the Mouse Deer and tells him he wants to eat him.

2. C The illustration does not fully represent the text because it isn't able to show how cunning the Mouse Deer is.

3. Part A- B. The moral is that cleverness is more important than size. The tiny Mouse Deer is able to outsmart the Tiger and stay safe. The other answer choices are incorrect.

Part B- B. The illustration does not support the moral because it doesn't show the cleverness of the Mouse Deer, which directly relates to the moral.

4. Example answer: A supporting illustration would likely show the deer mouse outsmarting the tiger, reinforcing the main idea that even small creatures can be the smartest and most clever.

5. A. This illustration shows that the hen has to do all the work on her own, even when the other animals could help, but choose not to. For example, the pig is sleeping in the background.

6. C. The illustration shows the Little Red Hen surrounded by the chicks she must care for. The other answer choices are not supported by the image.

7. C The illustration does not represent the text of the story because it doesn't show the other animals refusing to help. The picture doesn't match the tone of the passage.

8. Example answer: The moral of the text is: Only those who work can reap the rewards of that work. The image in question 5 most clearly connects to this moral, as it shows the hen working hard and the other animals refusing to participate.

RL.4.9 Compare & Contrast Themes/Events in Different Cultural Stories/Myths

1. A. The fox betrays the donkey but the consequence is that the lion gets them both.

2. C. A theme shared in both stories is "don't be too trusting." In Passage 1, the donkey trusts the fox and the lion, who both deceive him. And the fox trusts the lion, who deceives him. In Passage 2, the crow is so overcome with the fox's flattery that she lets her guard down.

3. B. This fable is about a flattering fox and a naive crow, and develops the theme that you should never trust anyone that flatters you for no reason.

4.

"The Donkey, The Fox, and the Lion"	"The Fox and the Crow"
Aesop uses the actions of multiple characters to explore the topic of deception.	Aesop has a character explicitly address the topic of deception by stating the moral.

5. B. Passage 1 uses third person narration to approach his topic/s. Passage 2 uses dialogue between the characters. The author doesn't use first person narration or setting to explore his topic/s.

6. Example answer: Passages 1 and 2 both detail how animals try to trick one another in order to get something they want. In Passage 1, the fox wants protection from the lion, so he proposes a deal. In Passage 2, the fox wants the cheese that the crow has. The plots end differently though. In Passage 1 the donkey does not stay safe. But in Passage 2, the fox gets the cheese after he conned the crow.

7. Part A- C. The pig uses his own fear to outsmart the wolf, and at the end, he is able get the wolf. The pig isn't originally trying to deceive, but is able to while trying to stay safe.

Part B- C. This passage details how the pig outsmarts the wolf. The other passages are irrelevant to the theme.

8. Example answer: The theme in the "Three Little Pigs" deals with one character tricking another character to achieve a goal. In this case, the pig tricks the wolf by getting in a barrel and rolling past him, and then by putting a pot of boiling water under the chimney to catch the wolf, thereby avoiding being eaten by the wolf. The themes in passage 1 and 2 also deal with with the same theme of deception and trickery where one character/s outsmarts or tricks another character/s to achieve a goal.

READING: INFORMATION

RI.4.1 Understand Text: Refer to Details and Draw Inferences

1. C. Humpback whales breach, which means they jump out of the water. While humpbacks are endangered, the article states that many types of whales are, so this isn't a unique feature. The other two answer choices are incorrect.

2. A. The law in 1966 probably helped humpbacks from becoming extinct. The article says that before the law hunting had reduced the population to just 1400, and since the law the number of humpbacks has increased.

3. D. The article lists three possible reasons for the song: attracting mates, showing authority or dominance over other males, and echolocation for finding food. Predators are not mentioned.

4. Sample answer: Humpback whales have a large body (40-50 feet long) with a hump. They breach by jumping out of the water when they breathe at the surface. The males sing a complicated song.

5. B. The songs are repeated in patterns. The other answer choices are incorrect.

6. D. Whales and humans are alike because they exchange culture. Whales pass song through nearby pods. Answer C may be true, but it does not answer the question directly like D. There is no evidence supporting B in the passage – that human sounds can be heard as far away as whale sounds.

7. Part A - A. Humpbacks switch between old and new songs at points in those songs where the melody sounds the same. The process is not random.

Part B –B. Part A is supported by the line in the article that discusses when humpbacks change between old and new songs (when they sound the same).

8. Students can find evidence in first paragraph and final paragraph to provide a strong answer for this question. Sample student answer: Humpback whales live in pods, and share their song among that pod. Nearby pods also share songs with one another. Humpback whales can hear the songs of other whales from 100 miles away. Therefore a pod can pass a song to another pod a hundred miles away, which passes it to another pod another hundred miles away. This means that, over time, a song can travel a long distance up to thousands of miles.

RI.4.2 Determine Main Idea & Summarize Text

1.B. The paragraph explains different features of Michael Phelps's body that make him a good swimmer. It is true that (D) he has big feet that act like flippers in the water, but this is not the main idea of the paragraph, rather a supporting detail. The information in answer choice C is not mentioned in paragraph 2. Choice A is not the main idea of paragraph 2, and contains information which is the opposite of the main idea of the whole passage.

2. A. The title questions who might be the greatest swimmer of all. Choice A answers this question by stating that the great white shark is the king of the seas. Other answer choices explain more about Michael's success as a swimmer, but don't relate directly to the title.

3. Part A- A. Choice A is correct. The majority of the passage gives supporting details for this central idea. The title and the final paragraph also indicates that this is the main idea. The first two paragraphs describe Michael Phelps's Olympic history and swimming ability, but this is not the key message of the passage. Choices C and D are true, but are only mentioned as details about Michael Phelps.

Part B - D. Choices A-C all give supporting details of the main idea that the great white shark was faster than Michael Phelps. Choice D is incorrect because it discusses how the race was set up, which does not support the main idea.

4. Example answer: Michael Phelps is one of the best swimmers of all times. His physical body and hard work helped him win for many years. He raced a great white shark, but the shark was faster.

5. A. Athletes who want to become the best must practice and train their minds and bodies. Answer choice C is true, but is not the main idea of the passage. There is no evidence for choice B in the passage. Choice D is incorrect as fans may want to see an exciting competition, but the passage does not say this is the reason that athletes train to be fast and strong. An exciting competition is a byproduct of athletes' intense training.

6. D. Athletes must be ready for distractions in competition so it doesn't hurt their performance. Other answer choices may be true, but do not answer the question directly like answer choice 'D'. Answer choice 'A' describes being in the zone during practice not competition.

7. Part A - B. Muscle memory is developed when a skill is practiced over and over.

Part B –B. Part A is supported by the line in the article that discusses how repeated practice is important for learning skills (Paragraph 4).

8. Students can find evidence in each paragraph to provide a strong answer for this question. Sample student answer: Athletes must practice well in order to perform well in competition. What an athlete learns by performing a move over and over during practice takes over in a competition. This is true for mental distractions and physical moves.

RI.4.3 Use Details to Explain Events, Procedures & Ideas in Text

1. A. The third paragraph explains that the flag was finished in June 1776 and the Declaration of Independence was signed the next month. While the other events all occurred, they did not occur immediately after the flag was finished.

2. B. Paragraph 2 states that the fabric business was struggling, due to lack of fabric in the time of war. Because of that, John Ross joined the war.

3. C. The text states that result of Betsy and John's marriage was that Betsy was rejected by her family and her church. The text shows that their marriage directly caused those events. The other answer choices are all facts, but none of them are directly caused by the marriage.

4. Example answer: The sewing of the first flag and the Declaration of Independence were both parts of the Revolutionary War. Betsy Ross was asked to sew the flag to show unity against Britain. The Declaration of Independence and the flag both helped build the new nation America, according to the text.

5. C. According to the text, the last part of production is when special effects are added. When preproduction begins, users test the game.

(paragraphs 4-5) The other answer choices are incorrect. Although the other answer choices do occur in the process, they do not happen immediately after production is finished.

6. A. All of the answer choices B-D are tasks completed by the preproduction team, according to paragraphs 2-3. Answer choice A occurs after the final product is ready.

7. Part A- A. The game is tested to make sure there are no errors, so it can be improved and become the best game possible.

Part B- B. Part A is supported by the line in the article that discusses how the engineer fixes issues (paragraph 5).

8. Students can find evidence in each paragraph to provide a strong answer for this question. [Sample answer: Video game production starts the storyboard and game design is done. Code is written by engineers and programmers. The team works on making the game perfect. Special effects are added.]

RI.4.4 Determine Word Meaning in Text

1. A. The word scorching most nearly means "hot." The other answer choices are incorrect. The meaning of the word can be inferred through the previous sentence, which describes the "searing heat of the desert."

2. B. The word radiate is used to describe how the fennec fox's ears pull heat away from its body. The other answer choices are incorrect.

3. D. Nocturnal is a domain-specific word that means that the fennec fox is active at night. Readers can infer its meaning because of the clause at the end of the sentence, "during the day."

4. Example answer: The author uses the word adaptive to describe the foxes because they have several characteristics that help them survive in the harsh desert climate. Their large ears radiate body heat, their fur protects them, and their nocturnal habits mean they miss the heat of day.

5. C. The prefix un means not, making the word unlike mean "not like."

6. A. The opposite of mild is "harsh." In the context of this article, mild refers to the fact that bats are not aggressive. "Gentle" would be a synonym. "Cautious" is unrelated. "Spicy" is an antonym of mild, and does not relate this context.

7. Part A- D. Twilight refers to the time when the sun goes down in the evening, so "sunset" is closest in meaning. The other answer choices are incorrect.

Part B- A and C. The phrase "flying through the dusky air" and "as night falls" helps the reader understand the meaning of twilight because dusk is a time when the sun is going down.

8. Example answer: The word distributing means spreading or scattering. You can use context clues to discover the meaning. The text says that bats eat flower nectar and fruit, both of which have seeds. The bat then moves these seeds to "different places," according to the text. This helps the reader know that the seeds are being spread or scattered.

RI.4.5 Describe Structure of Events, Ideas or Information in Text

1. B. A cold is caused by a virus that infects the nose and throat. Answer choices 'A' and 'C' are related to allergies, and answer choice 'D' is the result of of a cold, not a cause.

2. C. The text includes section headings that help the reader understand that colds and allergies are being compared. The other answer choices are incorrect.

3. A. The structure of the article is to compare and contrast allergies and colds. The other answer choices are incorrect.

4. Example answer: The article compares colds with allergies. Both have similar symptoms. Colds are caused by a virus that infects the nose or throat. Allergies are caused by the immune system's response to an allergen.

5. B. The article is in chronological order. The reader can tell because dates are used, and the life of Pelé is discussed from beginning to present.

6. The correct order of events is:

A. Pelé was born into a Brazilian family.
D. Pelé joined his first professional soccer team.
C. Pelé won his first World Cup.
F. Pelé became the biggest goal-scorer in history.
E. Pelé retired for the first time.
B. Pelé came out of retirement.

1. A
2. D
3. C
4. F
5. E
6. B

7. Part A- C. After his second retirement, Pelé became an ambassador for sports as a way to promote peace and understanding. While some other choices could be correct, the article does not mention them.

Part B- D. The only answer choice that directly relates to Pelé becoming an ambassador is that "He worked to promote peace and understanding through sports."

8. Example answer: This text is a chronological account of Pelé's life. It begins with his birth and continues until he retired from soccer the second time and became an ambassador. The article uses dates to help support the order of ideas.

RI.4.6 Compare & Contrast Firsthand & Secondhand Accounts

1. A. Passage 1 is a firsthand account because it is written by Helen Keller. The other answer choices are incorrect.

2. B. Passage 1 is written by Helen Keller. The reader knows this because of the title and because the narrator is describing the events that occur in first person. The other answer choices are incorrect.

3. D. Passage 2 emphasizes how Anne helps Helen understand the world around her. None of the other answer choices are accurate.

4. A. The details "Anne could sense that Helen didn't connect," and "With dramatic difficulty..." show that Anne had a difficult time helping Helen connect words and meanings.

5. Example answer: Both accounts describe how Helen Keller came to understand the world around her. The secondhand account gives more background (she was deaf/mute, unwilling to participate in the spelling game at first) that helps the reader understand the context of the event. The firsthand account, written by Helen, is full of imagery and helps the reader imagine how and what Helen felt during the event. It gives insight to Helen's emotions.

6. The correct answer is:

Passage 1: firsthand account, shows emotion, single, specific memory

Both: about Helen Keller, describes how Helen learned words

Passage 2: secondhand account, gives facts, background information

7. Part A- B. The first passage demonstrates Helen's emotions as only a firsthand account can.

Part B- C and D. These answer choices reveal Helen's emotions, about going outside and about her first experience with understanding. The other answer choices are not directly related to Helen's emotions.

8. Example answer: Helen was locked in her own world. Because she understood little, she threw tantrums. I began by giving her a doll, and spelling out d-o-l-l in her hand. She liked this at first, and I taught her other spellings. But I could tell she did not connect the doll in her hand to "doll" the word. We argued over "mug" and "water." I could tell she was smart, but I needed to help her brain connect. So I took her outside, to where water was running. I placed her hand under the running water and spelled w-a-t-e-r. Her face lit up! She now knew that the wetness running down her arm was water.

RI.4.7 Using Images/Diagrams to Understand Text

1. The correct order from least to greatest is:

Least — D — A — B — C — Most

2. C. The main objective is to compare glucose in drinks. Answer 'D' is too general. The other answer choices are incorrect.

3. A. Coca Cola and Energy Drink have the highest levels of glucose and the bar graph reaches the same point. The other answer choices are incorrect.

4. Example answer: Toby dipped a test strip into each beverage, then matched the color of the test strip to the color indicated for glucose concentration. Toby graphed each beverage according to the amount of glucose (per 20 ounces of liquid) to determine that Coca Cola and Energy Drink had the highest amount of glucose of those tested.

5. B. The musicians should register and then sit with their instrument section. This is given in the instructions at the top of the schedule. The other answer choices are incorrect.

6. C. The final rehearsal is at 3:00 pm. Readers can infer this even though it does not say "final rehearsal" on the schedule—it is the last listed rehearsal of the day.

7. Part A- A. If Ryan will take another 15 minutes to arrive, and it is 8:10, then Ryan will arrive at 8:25 am. That will allow him 5 minutes to register and make it to the first event on time.

Part B- D. Readers must infer that registration lasts until 8:30 since there is no other event until that time. The other answer choices are irrelevant to Part A.

8. Example answer: Kelly will miss the last part of Station 5 (try out a new instrument) and the beginning of Station 6 (Rehearse with your instrument family).

RI.4.8 Explain How Authors Use Evidence to Support Point of View

1. D. The author's main point is that humans copy nature to make our lives better. Answer choice A. The other answer choices are either unsupported by the text or not the author's main point.

2. A. Bicycle helmets are an example of a human invention inspired by nature that directly relates to safety. Answer choices B, C and D do not support the author's claim that nature helps us invent things for safety.

3. C. The author's purpose is to explain how many inventions come from nature. The other answer choices are unsupported by the text.

4. Example answer: The author could expand on the second adaptation mimicked from animals (camouflage), as it is mentioned but not explained. Also, the author could more clearly identify other human problems already solved through biomimicry. This would make her claim that humans imitate nature stronger.

5. A. The purpose of the article is education and to convince the reader of the dangers of cell phone use while driving. While the author does give information about the number of accidents caused by phone use, this is a detail of the passage, not the passage's main purpose. The author does not threaten. Answer choice 'D' is too general and not the main focus of the article.

6. B. Paragraph 4 emphasizes that even though people know cell phones are dangerous to use while driving, most people admit to using them while driving. The other answer choices are not the focus of the paragraph.

7. Part A- C. The main claim of the article is that driving while using a cell phone is dangerous. The other answer choices are incorrect or unsupported by the text.

Part B- C. This sentence shows that the reader is trying to convince her readers that using cell phones while driving is dangerous. The other answer choices are irrelevant to Part A.

8. Example answer: The author states that smart phones are even more dangerous than cell phones but does not support this with evidence. The author should include evidence showing why smart phones are more dangerous (they allow access to social media, email, etc.) in order to strengthen the claim.

RI.4.9 Integrate Information from Two Texts

1. C. The question posed in answer choice C. is answered in Passage 2 with the statement, "And eventually the movement started by just one woman helped to change segregation laws." The other choices are not directly answered in Passage 2.

2.

Important ideas about Rosa Parks	Both Passages	Passage 1	Passage 2
	Rosa Parks believed that it was unfair for blacks and whites to have separate seats.	Rosa Parks was tired after a long day's work when she decided not to move to the back of the bus.	Rosa Parks organized a car-pool system that helped African Americans boycott the bus for years.
Rosa Parks worked in politics, fighting against inequality.			

3. B. Parks lost her job and became ill as a result of her actions. The other answer choices are not direct results of her actions that affected her personally and negatively.

4. Example answer: Rosa Parks affected equality for African American people by taking a stand against segregation. She refused to give up her seat and was arrested. That caused an African American bus boycott, which she helped by organizing a car-pool for over a year. Eventually her actions and those of others helped to make segregation illegal.

5. The detail "She was the secretary" is the least important detail because it does not directly support the paragraph's main idea that Parks knew that something important had to happen to create change.

6. A. Passage 1 doesn't highlight the personal cost that Rosa Parks suffered for her actions. The other details in the answer choices are directly or indirectly touched on in Passage 1.

7. Part A- A. Segregation is the only idea of the four answer choices that is explained in detail in Passage 1.

Part B- C. This sentence gives an example of what segregation laws included. The other answer choices are irrelevant to Part A or do not support its answer.

8. Example answer: If I were writing about Rosa Parks' impact on equality, I would organize my information in a chart. I would list 1) Rosa Parks' beliefs and experiences before the bus incident, 2) Rosa Parks' actions on the bus, and 3) The results of the bus incident, both long term and short term. One thing the authors of Passages 1 and 2 did not include that I would include is information about what and when segregation laws changed.

LANGUAGE
L.4.1 Have Command of Grammar & Usage
L.4.1A

1. B. The word "who" is the relative pronoun, identifying that the girl stole the bike. The other answer choices are incorrect.

2. C. The word "who" is the correct relative pronoun, identifying the teacher as the person who helps us learn. Answer choice A should use "which" rather than "that." Choices B and D are incorrect.

3. A. "That" is the correct word to refer to the shoes Josie chose. The other answer choices are incorrect.

4. B. "That's talents" is correctly replaced by "whose talents," with the word "whose" functioning as a relative pronoun. The other answer choices are incorrect.

L.4.1B

1. B. "Is planning" is the present progressive tense. Answer choices A and C are not progressive tense, and answer choice D is future progressive tense.

2. A. The verb "is playing" does not match the preceding clause "last year" in tense. The other answer choices are correct.

3. D. Answer choice D shows past progressive tense through the phrase "I was walking." The other answer choices are incorrect.

4.

past progressive	I was swimming.
present progressive	I am swimming.
future progressive	I will be swimming.

L.4.1C

1. C. "Could" shows the past ability to do something. "Can" shows a present ability, while the other answer choices are conditional.

2. B. B is the only answer choice that correctly uses a modal auxiliary verb, stating that the branch could fall at any moment. The other answer choices are incorrect.

3. C. The missing word in the sentence is the word "must," showing that, in order for the speaker to pick up the subject, he or she has to provide information about how to get there. The other answer choices are incorrect.

4. B. Since Dan's parents have left him a choice, the word "can" correctly identifies the condition. The other answer choices are incorrect.

L.4.1D

1. A. The correct order of adjectives is article, number, opinion, size, age, shape, color, origin, material, and purpose. Answer choice A is the only sentence with adjectives in the correct order.

2. B. The correct order is: the (article) / old (age)/ wooden (material) rocking (purpose) chair (noun). The other answer choices are incorrect.

3. C. The correct order of the adjectives is huge (size), long (shape), brown (color). The other answer choices are incorrect.

4. B. The order is incorrect as black (color) should not come before long (shape). The other answer choices are correct.

L.4.1E

1. C. The preposition 'underneath' is correct in this sentence because it is describing a location and a single object. 'Between' is not correct as the sentence does not contain a description of multiple objects.

2. B. The prepositional phrase "of the book" starts with the preposition "of." The object of the preposition is "book."

3. C. Prepositions are words that connect a noun or pronoun to the rest of the sentence. The noun or pronoun after the preposition is the object of the preposition. In this sentence, the object of the preposition is the noun 'Morocco'.

4. B. Here, the correct preposition is "with."

5. D. "In" is the correct preposition. The prepositional phrase begins with "in" and ends with the object of the preposition "corner."

L.4.1F

1. C. This sentence is a run-on because it includes two complete thoughts (put on your helmet AND stay safe on your bike) with no conjunction or punctuation. The other answer choices are correct.

2. B. Answer choice B correctly edits the run-on sentence by creating two sentences out of the two thoughts. The other answer choices are incorrect.

3. B. Answer choice B adds the conjunction "so" to connect the two thoughts (the sun is hot AND wear sunscreen). Answer choice A revises the sentence with punctuation, not a conjunction. Choice C uses a conjunction incorrectly.

4. Part A: The bold sentence is a run-on sentence.

My dad needs to fix the water spout outside. **He says we need to start before it gets dark, the darkness will make it hard to see.** The sun is beginning to go down. I get my headlamp just in case we can't see.

Part B: [Answer: He says we need to start before it gets dark because the darkness will make it hard to see.]

L.4.1G

1. B. This sentence correctly uses the word "too" meaning "excessively."

2. C. The corrected sentence should read "There are two (the number of) dogs over there (location).

3. D. The correct sentence is "You're (you are) the best!" The other answer choices use the incorrect versions of frequently confused words.

4. **Where are you planning to spend your Christmas break?**

L. 4.2 Know Capitalization, Punctuation & Spelling

L.4.2A

1. C. The proper nouns in this sentence that should be capitalized are Joe (name), Soups & More

ANSWER EXPLANATIONS 119

(restaurant name), Arlington (city), and Virginia (state). No other nouns should be capitalized.

2. C. "Bakersville Elementary School" and "Mrs. Helgesen" should be capitalized because they are proper nouns. The other answer choices are correct.

3. D. "Sarah" is the only name or proper noun in the sentence so it should be capitalized.

4. Do you and Joshua remember the name of the store where we bought Kansas City souvenirs?

L.4.2B

1. B. Only the direct speech ("I think you have the wrong number" should be in quotation marks.

2. C. Sentence 3 is incorrect, because the entire sentence is in quotation marks. Only the direct speech should be: "I already did," I told him.

3. C. The comma belongs after the word 'wondering' and the word "said'. If the direct speech is broken up by information about who is speaking, you need a comma (or a question mark or exclamation mark) to end the first piece of speech and a full stop or another comma before the second piece (before the inverted comma or commas):

4. "Wow! What a great experience," said Dan. "I know I'll come back."

L.4.2C

1. A. A comma belongs after the coordinating conjunction in a sentence, in this case, the word "and." B has a comma after a conjunction, but the comma isn't needed because "and teasing one another" isn't an independent clause. The other answer choices are incorrect.

2. B. The comma belongs before the coordinating conjunction, "and."

3.

Independent Clause #1	Independent Clause #2	Coordinating Conjunction	Comma Placement
I'm practicing math every night	I can win the mathlete competition	so	after the word 'night'

4. [Charlie likes to listen to music on Pandora, but Cerise prefers to play games on a tablet.]

L.4.2D

1. B. The word "emphesized" should be spelled "emphasized." The other words are spelled correctly.

2. D. The word "catch" is the only correctly spelled word. The other words should be spelled "problem," "compass," and "except."

3. D. The word "villain" is correct as written.

4.

Word	Syllables
vocal	2
proposal	3
twelve	1
inverse	2
canopy	3

L.4.3 Use Appropriate Language Conventions To Convey Ideas

L.4.3A

1. B. The word "slithered" is more precise because it shows the intensity of the motion. The sentence mentions the boy is "desperate" which matches in intensity. 'Moved' is not more precise or descriptive than crawled.

2.

Least Intense → Moist → Soggy → Drenched → Most Intense

3. D. "wise" is the most precise way to replace the word "smart" in this sentence, especially due to the fact that it is talking about elders and advice. Although the other answer choices could potentially mean "smart," none correctly match the connotation.

4. Example answer: Intelligent refers to someone who has great knowledge and abilities. A person who is crafty is clever, or perhaps even sneaky.

L.4.3B

1. C. This sentence is correctly identified as an exclamation, punctuated by an exclamation point. Some context clues in the sentence show that it is not simply a statement: "oh dear", "favorite" and "completely ruined."

2. A. This sentence is a statement, punctuated by a period. There are no context clues to make the reader think it's an exclamation, and question and command are incorrect choices.

3. A. Quotation marks go around the spoken dialogue. The question mark is included inside of the quotation marks because it is part of the dialogue (the dialogue asks a question).

4. Example answer: "Oh no, what am I going to do

about this science project?" or "Oh no—what am I going to do about this science project?"

L.4.3C

1. D. This is the example of informal English, primarily because of the use of the slang term "gonna."

2. C. This is the example of formal English as it uses academic vocabulary. The other answer choices are informal.

3.

Informal	Formal
What's up?	How are you?
anyways	nevertheless
blow up	explode

4. Sample letter:

12/1/2017

Mr. Johns

Tall Tree Elementary School

1234 Learning Lane

New York, New York 12345

Dear Mr. Johns,

I believe that every student in our school should have access to an iPad. It is important to understand technology in today's academic environment. iPads are a helpful tool for learning skills like coding. Furthermore, if every student had an iPad, we could increase instructional time for the teacher. Thank you for considering my request.

Sincerely,
Keisha

L.4.4 Determine Meaning of Unknown Words When Reading

L.4.4A

1. Part A- C. The word "wealthy" means "rich."

Part B- The text explains that the man married a rich wife and became wealthy. This serve as a context clue for the meaning of "wealthy."

2. C. The word "distinguished" means "saw" based on the detail that Ali Baba could see the body of horsemen.

3. Ali Baba, who expected a dark, dismal cavern, was surprised to see a well-lighted and spacious chamber, which received the light from an opening at the top of the rock, and in which were all sorts of provisions, <u>bales of silk, brocade, and carpeting, piled upon one another, gold and silver ingots in great heaps, and money in bags</u>. The sight of all these <u>riches</u> made him suppose that this cave must have been occupied for ages by robbers, who had succeeded one another.

4.

My Definition	My Sentence
Provisions are things like supplies of food or clothing or equipment.	If you are going camping, you want to be sure to pack some **provisions,** including sturdy camping gear, food, drink or any other necessary supplies.

L.4.4B

1. B. Dismounted means that he climbed off of his horse. Without the prefix, it would say that he mounted, or climbed on. However, the prefix dis- means "apart," which changes the meaning.

2.

Prefix	Meaning	My Word	My Definition
mis-	ill/ incorrect	mistake	a wrong action
inter-	between	intermission	a time between to acts of a play or show
pre-	before	preschool	a school for kids before kindergarten stars
re-	again	repeat	to say again

3. D The suffix -ation means action. In the sentence, this can be see in the word "determination" (the action of being determined), capitalization (the action of capitalizing) and "reputation" (the action of being trustworthy or reputable).

4. Example answer: If the prefix "mis," meaning "ill" is taken away from the word "misfortune," it would imply that something good has happened to Cassim.

L.4.4C

1. "The grandchildren's inheritance means that they can afford college." This is the only answer choice that uses the word "inheritance" appropriately because it shows that the children will gain money from a relative to afford something (college).

2. B. [spey-shuh s] is the correct part of the dictionary entry to show the pronunciation of spacious.

3.

Word:	conceal
Pronunciation	[kuh n-**seel**]
Part of Speech	verb
Meaning/Definition	to hide

4. B. This is the correct use of the word "due" as an adjective because it shows that they are expected to arrive at a certain time. Answer choices A and D use the noun form and answer choice C uses the adverb form.

L4.5 Understand Figurative Language
L.4.5A

1. B. The simile is "as muddy as pig's hooves" because it compares the boy's boots to something that shares a common feature (pig's hooves).

2. A. The metaphor compares the wave to a crumbling wall, showing its height and impact.

3. D. The simile "flat as a pancake" compares the boy's feelings to the flattened snowman.

4. Example response: The girl's eyes are as blue as the sea like her mother's eyes.

L.4.5B

1. B. The idiom "having second thoughts" means that a person is having doubts.

2. A. The word "dog" correctly completes the adage "You can't teach an old dog new tricks."

3. C. The word "bird" correctly completes the adage "Birds of a feather flock together."

4. Example response: The adage a penny saved is a penny earned means that money that you save is more valuable than money that you spend right away. It means it is good to save money. It means that it is as useful to save money that you already have as it is to earn more money.

L.4.5C

1. B. The word "disobedient" means that Aladdin didn't listen to his father and mother. Therefore, it's antonym is "respectful," which would imply that he did listen.

2. Part A- A. The word "disappointed" reveals that the grade was not good.

Part B- B. Therefore, the opposite meaning of the word "atrocious" is "excellent."

3. C. All of the answer choices EXCEPT C (indifferent) could be used as a synonym for the word happy.

4.

Synonyms of Small	Antonyms of Small
1. miniature	1. enormous
2. slight	2. huge
3. little	3. big
4. tiny	4. large

L.4.6 Know & Use General Academic/ Domain-Specific Words

1. B. The word "harmony" means "stability." The passage talks about how the ecosystem must be in balance, or stable, when referring to its harmony.

2. A. The phrase "everything works together" provides a context clue for the meaning of "balance," referring to how living and non-living things live together in harmony.

3. C. The word "interact" can be replaced with the word "cooperate." Thai can be inferred from the context clues in the passage that show that the ecosystem needs living and non-living things to stay in balance.

4. Example response: Stability- the balance or steadiness of how living and non-living things interact.

5. C. This blank is best replaced with the word "assured." Julie is trying to convince her mom that she is fine.

6. A. This blank is best replaced with the word "concentrate." The context clue "Paying attention was a chore" provides the reader with this information.

7. B. This blank is best replaced with the word "embarrassment." This is supported by the context clue in the previous sentence that Julie was mortified.

8. B. The word "pounded" shows how badly Julie's headache hurts. The other answer choices are incorrect.

9. D. The word "investigate" can be replaced with the word "research." Galileo wanted to perform experiments to discover how and why his theories worked.

10.

Word: principles	Definition: a truth or rule about how something works
Context Clue 1	"investigate those theories"
Context Clue 2	"apply them in everyday life"

OPERATIONS & ALGEBRAIC THINKING

PRACTICE TESTS

ELA ASSESSMENT
Grade 4

PRACTICE TEST ONE
Session 1
(Reading)

Directions: Read the passage, then answer the questions below.

Excerpt from Peter Pan
by J.M. Barrie

Feeling that Peter was on his way back, the Neverland had again woke into life. We ought to use the pluperfect and say wakened, but woke is better and was always used by Peter.

In his absence things are usually quiet on the island. The fairies take an hour longer in the morning, the beasts attend to their young, the redskins feed heavily for six days and nights, and when pirates and lost boys meet they merely bite their thumbs at each other. But with the coming of Peter, who hates lethargy, they are all under way again; if you put your ear to the ground now, you would hear the whole island seething with life.

seething = filled

On this evening the chief forces of the island were disposed as follows. The lost boys were out looking for Peter, the pirates were out looking for the lost boys, the redskins were out looking for the pirates, and the beasts were out looking for the redskins. They were going round and round the island, but they did not meet because all were going at the same rate.

disposed = busy doing something

All wanted blood except the boys, who liked it as a rule, but tonight were out to greet their captain. The boys on the island vary, of course, in numbers, according as they get killed and so on; and when they seem to be growing up, which is against the rules, Peter thins them out; but at this time there was six of them, counting the twins as two. Let us pretend to lie here among the sugar-cane and watch them as they steal by in single file, each with his hand on his dagger.

They are forbidden by Peter to look in the least like him, and they wear the skins of bears slain by themselves, in which they are so round and furry that when they fall they roll. They have therefore become very sure-footed.

slain = killed

The first to pass is Tootles, not the least brave but the most unfortunate of all that gallant band. He had been in fewer adventures than any of them, because the big things constantly happened just when he had stepped round the corner; all would be quiet, he would take the opportunity of going off to gather a few sticks for firewood, and then when he returned the others would be sweeping up the blood. This ill-luck had

gallant = daring and brave

given a gentle melancholy to his countenance, but instead of souring his nature had sweetened it, so that he was quite the humblest of the boys. Poor kind Tootles, there is danger in the air for you tonight. Take care lest an adventure is now offered you, which, if accepted, will plunge you in deepest woe. Tootles, the fairy Tink who is bent on mischief this night is looking for a tool, and she thinks you the most easily tricked of the boys. 'Ware Tinker Bell.

melancholy = sadness

countenance = face

woe = trouble

Would that he could hear us, but we are not really on the island, and he passes by, biting his knuckles.

Next comes Nibs, the gay and debonair, followed by Slightly, who cuts whistles out of the trees and dances ecstatically to his own tunes. Slightly is the most conceited of the boys. He thinks he remembers the days before he was lost, with their manners and customs, and this has given his nose an offensive tilt. Curly is fourth; he is a pickle, and so often has he had to deliver up his person when Peter said sternly, "Stand forth the one who did this thing," that now at the command he stands forth automatically whether he has done it or not. Last come the Twins, who cannot be described because we should be sure to be describing the wrong one. Peter never quite knew what twins were, and his band were not allowed to know anything he did not know, so these two were always vague about themselves, and did their best to give satisfaction by keeping close together in an apologetic sort of way.

debonair = charming and light-hearted

conceited = to think too highly of oneself

deliver up his person = own up

The boys vanish in the gloom, and after a pause, but not a long pause, for things go briskly on the island, come the pirates on their track. We hear them before they are seen, and it is always the same dreadful song:

Avast belay, yo ho, heave to,

A-pirating we go,

And if we're parted by a shot

We're sure to meet below!

1. Which of the following traits best describes Peter?
   - **A.** a leader
   - **B.** a follower
   - **C.** unsure
   - **D.** thoughtless

PRACTICE TEST ONE

2. Which piece of evidence from the text supports the answer to Part A?
   A. "The first to pass is Tootles, not the least brave but the most unfortunate of all that gallant band."
   B. "We ought to use the pluperfect and say wakened, but woke is better and was always used by Peter."
   C. "Let us pretend to lie here among the sugar-cane and watch them as they steal by in single file, each with his hand on his dagger."
   D. "All wanted blood except the boys, who liked it as a rule, but tonight were out to greet their captain."

3. The theme of this excerpt can be summarized as:
   A. Leaders have a great influence on their followers.
   B. It is better to be a follower than a leader.
   C. All children are followers.
   D. Peter Pan is a terrible leader.

4. Identify a selection from this text that **best** supports the answer to Part A.
   A. "Feeling that Peter was on his way back, the Neverland had again woke into life."
   B. "Would that he could hear us, but we are not really on the island, and he passes by, biting his knuckles."
   C. "The fairies take an hour longer in the morning, the beasts attend to their young, the redskins feed heavily for six days and nights, and when pirates and lost boys meet they merely bite their thumbs at each other."
   D. "Take care lest an adventure is now offered you, which, if accepted, will plunge you in deepest woe."

5. What word or phrase could be used to substitute the word *lethargy* in paragraph 2?
   A. energy
   B. sadness
   C. laziness
   D. hard work

6. This excerpt is an example of which type of writing?
   A. drama
   B. prose
   C. poetry
   D. meter

Directions: Read the passages, then answer the questions below.

Passage 1: Sunny Star Up
Wish Upon the Sun

Have you ever wished upon a star? If you have, chances are that you did so during the nighttime. For it is only when the sun sets that we are able to view, with the naked eye, some of the billions of stars in our solar system. However, have you ever considered wishing upon the star that is in the center of our **solar system**? A solar system consists of a star and all the objects that travel around it. The sun is the center of the Earth's solar system. Therefore, when you wish upon a star, you can actually wish upon the sun!

How Did the Sun Form?

Before you can understand what the sun is composed of, it is important to know when and how the sun first formed. The Earth's solar system was created about five billion years ago. First, there existed a **nebula**. A nebula is a gigantic ball made of gas, dust, and ice. Next, the nebula's gravity was so strong that it pulled parts of the ball inside, toward the middle of itself. This force of gravity caused the ball to collapse and it began to spin. Then, the matter in the center of the ball increased exponentially in temperature. As a result, the sun formed. Meanwhile, the remaining dust, gas, and ice started to bunch together. These clumps would eventually form some of the solar system's comets, asteroids, planets, and moons.

Sun Size

The sun is so big that it's difficult to comprehend its size. The **diameter** of the sun is nearly 865,000 million miles. The diameter is the distance from one side of the sun to the other side of the sun. The Earth only has a diameter of approximately 8,000 miles. This means that about 1,000,000 Earths could fit inside the sun!

The sun sounds as though it's unimaginably large. However, it's actually considered a medium-sized star compared to the rest of the stars in the solar system. Some stars are even bigger than the sun. These stars are called **supergiants**. Supergiants can have diameters that are thousands of times bigger than the sun.

How Does the Sun Get So Hot?

Just like different levels of the ocean have different temperatures, different parts of the sun have different temperatures as well. For example, the part of the sun that is visible to earth measures about 10,000°F. However, at the core of the sun, temperatures can be as high as 27 million°F.

Why is the core of the sun so much hotter than the surface of the sun? The gas particles that make up the sun are packed closest together at the sun's center. This causes the particles to constantly crash into each other, forming heat and light energy. This process is called **nuclear fusion**. In this process, hydrogen changes into helium, creating the heat and light that all living beings on Earth depend on for survival.

Earth and Sun

Without the sun, life on Earth could not exist. For example, plants need the sun's light in order to make food. Animals, including humans, depend on plants for food. Additionally, the sun's heat keeps most of Earth's water in a liquid state, making water easily accessible to most living beings. The Earth also relies on the sun's energy. For instance, **solar energy** is becoming more and more popular. Solar energy is created by special equipment that transforms the sun's energy into electricity.

Significance of Our Sun Star

While the sun appears to be an ordinary star in regard to its size and place in the solar system, it is truly significant in many other ways. Most importantly, life on Earth would not exist without the sun. There would be no animals, no plants, no people, and no water. Think about it. The sun is the most important star in the Earth's solar system. Perhaps, instead of wishing upon a star next time you see one, you might thank the Earth's most important star for all it does and provides.

Passage 2: The Earth's Best Friend
Life on Earth

The Earth is the third farthest planet from the sun. The Earth is also the only planet known to have human life. The primary factor for this truth is the Earth's placement and relationship to the sun. The sun provides the perfect amount of heat, light, and energy that allow for life to exist and sustain here on Earth.

Star Structure

It may be hard to believe that Earth relies so heavily on a star. Yes, that's right. The sun is a star. The sun is basically a ball of hot gas that formed nearly five billion years ago. It has two basic regions, an inner and outer region. The outer region is composed of three main layers: the photosphere, the chromosphere, and the corona. The corona is the outermost layer of the sun. The chromosphere lies between the corona and the photosphere. The photosphere is the inner most part of the sun's atmosphere, and it is the only part of the sun that can be seen from Earth.

The inner region of the sun is also composed of three zones: the convective zone, the radiative zone, and the core. The convective zone is the outermost zone. The radiative zone surrounds the core, and the core is the centermost and hottest part of the sun.

The Sun's Gifts

The process of nuclear fusion creates the necessary gases the Earth needs in order to survive. During nuclear fusion, hydrogen is changed into helium. As a result, heat and light are emitted and transferred to Earth.

Internal structure:
inner core
radiative zone
convection zone
Subsurface flows
Photosphere
Chromosphere
Corona

First and foremost, heat and light ensure the sustainment of the water cycle. Heat is needed to transform liquid water into vapor gas, causing evaporation. Evaporation then allows for the rest of the water cycle to occur. All living beings on Earth, animals, plants, humans, need water to survive.

The Earth also needs the sun's light in order for life to exist. Plants use the sun's energy to make food through a process called photosynthesis. This is important because people and animals depend on plants for food.

The sun also gives the Earth its four seasons. As the Earth orbits the sun, different parts of the Earth experience different seasons. For example, summer occurs when a portion of the planet is closest to the sun. The changing of seasons also impacts what and when various types of crops can grow.

Water, energy, food, seasons, and life. These are just four of the countless gifts the sun gives to the Earth. In this way, the sun is, without a doubt, the Earth's best friend.

7. What topic is more fully explained by Passage 1 **(Sunny Star Up)** than by Passage 2 **(The Earth's Best Friend)**?

    A. the layers of the Earth
    B. the sun's benefits on Earth
    C. how the sun was created
    D. how the Earth was created

8. Which detail from the text supports the answer in question 7?
    A. "All living beings on Earth, animals, plants, humans, need water to survive."
    B. "In this process, hydrogen changes into helium, creating the heat and light that all living beings on Earth depend on for survival."
    C. "The sun is the center of the Earth's solar system."
    D. "Next, the nebula's gravity was so strong that it pulled parts of the ball inside, toward the middle of itself."

9. What is an effect of nuclear fusion?
    A. the sun is born
    B. light and heat are emitted from the sun
    C. the sun makes food for the Earth
    D. the gas particles are close together

10. What are supergiants?
    A. another name for the sun
    B. stars bigger than the sun
    C. planets bigger than the Earth
    D. planets bigger than the sun

11. Which of the following is NOT a detail about the sun?
    A. It would take 1,000,000 Earths to fit inside the sun.
    B. The diameter of the sun is 865,000 miles wide.
    C. The temperature of the sun's core is 27 million °F.
    D. The sun has only two layers.

12. Read the following paragraph from Passage 2 **(The Earth's Best Friend)**. Then follow the directions.

The process of nuclear fusion creates the necessary gases the Earth needs in order to survive. During nuclear fusion, hydrogen is changed into helium. As a result, heat and light are emitted and transferred to Earth.

Which of these words is the closest in meaning of the underlined word, emitted?
    A. hidden
    B. released
    C. kept
    D. combined

134 PRACTICE TEST ONE

Directions: Read the passage, then answer the questions below.

Excerpt from Black Beauty: The Autobiography of a Horse
by Anna Sewell

Every one may not know what breaking in is, therefore I will describe it. It means to teach a horse to wear a saddle and bridle, and to carry on his back a man, woman or child; to go just the way they wish, and to go quietly. Besides this he has to learn to wear a collar, a crupper, and a breeching, and to stand still while they are put on; then to have a cart or chaise fixed behind, so that he cannot walk or trot without dragging it after him; and he must go fast or slow, just as his driver wishes. He must never start at what he sees, nor speak to other horses, not bite, nor kick, nor have any will of his own, but always do his master's will, even though he may be very tired or hungry; but the worst of all is, when his harness is once on, he may neither jump for joy nor lie down for weariness. So you see this breaking in is a great thing.

I had of course been used to a halter and a headstall, and to be led about in the fields and lanes quietly, but now I was to have a bit and bridle; my master gave me some oats as usual, and after a good deal of coaxing he got the bit into my mouth, and the bridle fixed, but it was a nasty thing! Those who have never had a bit in their mouths cannot think how bad it feels; a great piece of cold hard steel as thick as a man's finger to be pushed into one's mouth, between one's teeth, and over one's tongue, with the ends coming out at the corner of your mouth, and held fast there by straps over your head, under your throat, round your nose, and under your chin; so that no way in the world can you get rid of the nasty hard thing; it is very bad! Yes, very bad! At least I thought so; but I knew my mother always wore one when she went out, and all horses did when they were grown up; and so, what with the nice oats, and what with my master's pats, kind words, and gentle ways, I got to wear my bit and bridle.

Next came the saddle, but that was not half so bad; my master put it on my back very gently, while old Daniel held my head; he then made the girths fast under my body, patting and talking to me all the time; then I had a few oats, then a little leading about; and this he did every day till I began to look for the oats and the saddle. At length, one morning, my master got on my back and rode me round the meadow on the soft grass. It certainly did feel queer; but I must say I felt rather proud to carry my master, and as he continued to ride me a little every day I soon became accustomed to it.

13. According to the text, what is one purpose of "breaking in" a horse?
    A. to harm it
    B. to make it tired and hungry
    C. to teach it to carry a rider
    D. to make it ready for a show

14. In the text, Black Beauty feels breaking in is:
    A. necessary
    B. harmful
    C. cruel
    D. exciting

15. Reread the following sentence.

"He must never start at what he sees, nor speak to other horses, not bite, nor kick, nor have any will of his own, but always do his master's will." (paragraph 1)

What is the closest meaning of the word "start" in this context?
    A. startle
    B. begin
    C. wander
    D. fatigue

16. Which phrase in paragraph one **best** provides a context clue for meaning of the word "start?"
    A. "to wear a saddle"
    B. "and to go quietly"
    C. "so that he cannot walk or trot without dragging it"
    D. "this breaking in is a great thing"

17. How does Black Beauty feel toward the master?
    A. appreciation for the master's gentleness
    B. hatred for the master for breaking her in
    C. fear of disappointing the master
    D. love of being ridden by the master

18. Which character trait best describes Black Beauty?
   A. Naughty
   B. Energetic
   C. Careful
   D. Obedient

19. Which sentence from the text in the list below provides the best evidence for the character trait you chose in Question 18?
   A. "...so that no way in the world can you get rid of the nasty hard thing; it is very bad!"
   B. "...but I knew my mother always wore one when she went out, and all horses did when they were grown up; and so, what with the nice oats, and what with my master's pats, kind words, and gentle ways, I got to wear my bit and bridle."
   C. "Every one may not know what breaking in is, therefore I will describe it. It means to teach a horse to wear a saddle and bridle..."
   D. "...he then made the girths fast under my body, patting and talking to me all the time;"

Directions: Read the passage, then answer the questions below.

The Navajo Nation

Hogans. Weaving. Southwest. Corn. What do all of these words have in common? Each of these words can be traced to the Navajo Native Americans. The Navajo lived in the southwestern deserts of the United States. Desert habitats have limited access to rain and water and no access to important resources such as buffalo and fish. However, the Navajo people learned how to adapt to the harsh conditions of the desert. Living in the desert impacted the types of homes the Navajo lived in, the kinds of food they had access to, the kinds of clothing they made and wore, and the kind of work they had to do in order to survive.

Desert Dwellers

The beginning of Navajo history can be traced all the way back to 1400. Believe it or not, hundreds of thousands of Navajo Native Americans are still alive today! Despite the Navajo's deadly battles with European settlers and losing much of its land to the United States Government, the Navajo Indian Reservation continues to be located in the southwestern deserts of the United States. Unfortunately, the reservation does not cover nearly the extent of land that the Navajo once inhabited. Today, the Navajo Indian Reservation is located at the borders of Arizona, New Mexico, Utah, and Colorado and spreads across approximately 25,000 square miles.

Shelter

While the majority of today's Navajo live in modern houses, this wasn't always the case. The traditional Navajo house is called a hogan. Hogans were one-room houses, usually occupying one family. Hogans were convenient for living in the desert habitat because they were composed of mud and logs. As a result of being built entirely from mud and logs, hogans kept cool in the summer, but also retained warmth during the colder, winter months. Hogans were shaped like domes and contained a door on the east side. Hogans didn't have any windows, but there was a hole in the roof that allowed for the proper exhaust of the fire pit that sat in the center of the home. The fire pit was typically utilized for cooking. There was no furniture on the hogan, so families slept on sheepskins around the fire.

Food

The unique climate of the desert makes it difficult to access particular animals, vegetables, and fruit. Furthermore, water is very limited. Therefore, the weather affected the food that the Navajo grew, hunted, and ate. The most important Navajo food was corn. The Navajo also grew squash and beans. Together, corn, squash, and beans is known as "The Three Sisters". In addition to vegetables, the Navajo did raise some livestock, such as sheep, goats, and horses, for food. Some of the Navajo living on the Navajo Indian Reservation today still farm and raise livestock today. For example, some Navajo raise goats, horses, cattle, and sheep.

Clothing

The desert climate also impacted the kind of clothing the Navajo made and wore. The Navajo are well known for their weaving. Sheep were an important resource to make weaving successful. First, the Navajo raised the sheep. Next, they sheared the wool from the sheep. After that, they spun the wool into yarn. The yarn was then dyed with plants and berries to make different colors. Last, they used a wooden loom to weave the wool. The final product could be anything from a skirt or breech cloth to a rug or blanket. Weaving is still an important part of Navajo life today.

Work

Men and women had different roles in the Navajo tribe. The men were primarily responsible for hunting, making hunting weapons, and protecting the family. On the other hand, women took on the roles of cooking, weaving, harvesting crops, and raising the children. It was important for the men and women to work together and to share the workload so that the family could survive and be well. Some Navajo women still make a living from making crafts and weaving today. Navajo people also hold more modern jobs such as teachers and police officers.

Native Americans Are Today's Americans

Many people relate Native Americans to the history or the past. They don't realize that many Native Americans still exist today! While much of the culture has adapted to fit today's standards of society, the majority of the heart of what makes each tribe unique still exists today.

20. Which of the following is not a food that the Navajo traditionally ate?
    A. corn
    B. squash
    C. goats
    D. buffalo

21. What is a main idea of paragraph 2?
    A. The Navajo have always lived in the desert.
    B. Only the Navajo Native Americans live in the desert.
    C. It is easy for the Navajo to live in the desert.
    D. Living in a desert environment is difficult.

22. Which detail from the text **best** supports your answer to Question 21?
    A. "The beginning of Navajo history can be traced all the way back to 1400."
    B. "Unfortunately, the reservation does not cover nearly the extent of land that the Navajo once inhabited."
    C. "... the Navajo Indian Reservation continues to be located in the southwestern deserts of the United States."
    D. "Believe it or not, hundreds of thousands of Navajo Native Americans are still alive today!"

23. Why was a hogan a useful shelter for desert living?
    A. A hogan was easy to make.
    B. Hogans protected the Navajo from the rain.
    C. Hogans kept warm in the winter and cool in the summer.
    D. Hogans could fit many people inside them.

24. What is the overall structure of paragraph 5?
    A. chronological
    B. sequential
    C. problem and solution
    D. compare and contrast

State ELA ASSESSMENT
Grade 4

Session 2
(Writing)

Directions: Read the passage, then answer the questions below.

Excerpt from Little Women
by Louisa May Alcott

It was well for all that this peaceful time was given them as preparation for the sad hours to come; for, by-and-by, Beth said the needle was "so heavy," and put it down forever; talking wearied her, faces troubled her, pain claimed her for its own, and her tranquil spirit was sorrowfully perturbed by the ills that vexed her feeble flesh. Ah me! Such heavy days, such long, long nights, such aching hearts and imploring prayers, when those who loved her best were forced to see the thin hands stretched out to them so beseechingly, to hear the bitter cry, "Help me, help me!" and to feel that there was no help. A sad eclipse of the serene soul, a sharp struggle of the young life with death, but both were mercifully brief, and then, the natural rebellion over, the old peace returned more beautiful than ever. With the wreck of her frail body, Beth's soul grew strong, and though she said little, those about her felt that she was ready, saw that the first pilgrim called was likewise the fittest, and waited with her on the shore, trying to see the Shining Ones coming to receive her when she crossed the river.

perturbed = upset

vexed = irritated

beseechingly = begging desperately

Jo never left her for an hour since Beth had said, "I feel stronger when you are here." She slept on a couch in the room, waking often to renew the fire, to feed, lift, or wait upon the patient creature who seldom asked for anything, and "tried not to be a trouble." All day she haunted the room, jealous of any other nurse, and prouder of being chosen then than of any honor her life ever brought her. Precious and helpful hours to Jo, for now her heart received the teaching that it needed: lessons in patience were so sweetly taught her that she could not fail to learn them; charity for all, the lovely spirit that can forgive and truly forget unkindness, the loyalty to duty that makes the hardest easy, and the sincere faith that fears nothing, but trusts undoubtingly.

Often when she woke Jo found Beth reading in her well-worn little book, heard her singing softly, to beguile the sleepless night, or saw her lean her face upon her hands, while slow tears dropped through the transparent fingers; and Jo would lie watching her with thoughts too deep for tears, feeling that Beth, in her simple, unselfish way, was trying to wean herself from the dear old life, and fit herself for the life to come, by sacred words of comfort, quiet prayers, and the music she loved so well.

beguile = to charm

25. What inference can you make about the relationship between Jo and Beth? Explain your answer using **two** pieces evidence from the passage.

26. What does the author mean when she says, "…in her simple, unselfish way, was trying to wean herself from the dear old life, and fit herself for the life to come…"? Use **two** pieces of evidence from the passage to support your answer.

PRACTICE TEST ONE 143

Directions: Read the passage, then answer the questions below.

That's A Tall Order

It was a cloudy, August morning in 1974. A thin tightrope weighing approximately 450 pounds lay between the North and South Towers of the World Trade Center in New York City. A quarter mile high into the sky, a man by the name of Philippe Petit was preparing to take one of the most dangerous walks of his life.

Petit's Childhood
Philippe Petit was born on August 13, 1949 in Nemours, Seine-et-Marne, France. Petit was fascinated by circus arts such as juggling and magic from a young age. As a child, he would perform these acts for tourists on the streets. It wasn't until the age of 16 that Petit began exploring the high wire and tightrope walking. After a year of training, tightrope walking was incorporated into Petit's street performance acts.

How It All Started
Not exactly a rule follower, Petit was kicked out of a handful of schools by the time he was 18 years old. This trend of character would continue into adulthood as Petit began to explore more menacing and treacherous acts. The first delinquent act that Petit pulled was in 1971 when he illegally walked on a wire between the towers of the Notre-Dame Cathedral in Paris, France. Subsequently, in 1973, he walked between the pylons of Sydney Harbor Bridge in Australia. However, Petit was never truly satiated with these stunts and continued to pursue something more.

Planning and Preparation
Petit recalls first learning about the construction of the Twin Towers when he was reading a magazine in the waiting room of a dentist's office. He was immediately captivated by the allure of possibly utilizing the two towers as a tight walking opportunity. From that day forward, Petit made a point to learn as much about the Twin Towers as he could. He collected articles, conducted research, and even visited the Twin Towers in January of 1974. Petit even closely observed the clothing of the construction workers and carried the identification of an American worker so that he and the members of his team could disguise themselves in order to gain access to the Twin Towers. Petit and his collaborators snuck into the towers several times to study everything from the roofs and building layout to information regarding security measures. In between his devious trips into the twin towers, Petit replicated the landscape of the Twin Towers and simulated the tight walking experience. For example, he laid a 200-ft. wire across a field in France and walked day after day with his 26 ft. long balancing pole. For the duration of 6 years, Petit carefully planned, prepared, and practiced for what would become one of the most dangerous and risk-taking stunts he would ever perform. He could leave no stone unturned.

On the evening of August 6, 1974, Petit and his team, disguised as construction workers, trudged up 104 flights up stairs to the roof of the South Tower with hundreds of pounds of equipment in hand. The men worked together to situate the steel cable across from the South Tower to the North Tower. This was only successful after many failed attempts with practice props such as fishing line and a bow and arrow. After several hours of manual, arduous labor, Petit was finally equipped and ready to walk.

The Walk

Shortly after 7:00 in the morning, Philippe Petit took his first steps from the South Tower onto the steel cable connected to the North Tower. With his 50-pound balancing pole in hand, 1,350 feet above the ground, Petit's stunt quickly attracted the attention of city onlookers below. Philippe walked back and forth between the towers 8 times. He even danced, lay down, and kneeled on the wire as larger crowds of people formed and cheered Philippe on. As Petit continued his daredevil performance, numerous police officers tried to persuade him to get off the wire. However, Petit continued his aerial tricks for 45 minutes before ceasing. Waiting for him on the other side was the police ready with handcuffs.

Consequences

Philippe Petit was ultimately arrested under various charges of trespassing and additional criminal acts related to his high wire walk. However, these charges were dropped and Petit did not have to serve any jailtime. After the twin towers stunt, Petit was requested to perform a free tightrope walking act for the city's children in Central Park. While the Twin Towers no longer stand, Petit's courageous walk between the towers will always stand as one of history's greatest tightrope performances of all time.

27. Read the following sentence from the passage (paragraph 4).

"He could leave no stone unturned."

According to the text, what does the phrase "leave no stone unturned" mean? Use **two** details from the story to support the answer in Part A.

PRACTICE TEST ONE   145

28. Summarize the text from beginning to end in a few sentence.

___

Directions: Read the passage, then answer the questions below.

An Evil Daredevil

A daredevil is someone who thrives on danger and risk-taking challenges. Daredevils pay no mind to the possible consequences of partaking in such tasks, be it a minor scratch or bruise or something much more severe such as a life-threatening injury. Robert Craig Knievel was one such stuntman.

Early Life

Born on October 17, 1938 in Butte, Montana, Robert Craig Knievel was attracted to danger from a young age. After dropping out of high school as a sophomore, Knievel took a job working in the copper mines as a drill operator. Knievel was eventually fired from his job when he tried to perform a motorcycle trick, called a wheelie, with the company's bulldozer. This resulted in Knievel crashing into the town's power lines, leaving the town of Butte without electricity for many hours.

Evel is Born

Without a job, Knievel had even more time on his hands to get into trouble. In 1956, Knievel, on his motorcycle, led police on a highspeed cheese which ended with him crashing his motorcycle. Knievel was jailed on reckless driving charges. It was during his jailtime that the nickname Evel Knievel was born.

A Daredevil is Born

Knievel first started performing motorcycle stunts in an effort to make money to support his struggling family. In his first show, Knievel attempted to jump a 20-ft. long box of rattlesnakes and two mountain lions. While Knievel landed short, hitting the box of rattlesnakes, he managed to land safely.

Knievel and His Motorcycle Daredevils debuted on January 3, 1966 at the National Date Festival in Indio, California. During this performance, Knievel used his motorcycle to perform wheelies, crash through plywood walls, and to jump over two firetrucks. Immediately, offers came pouring in for Knievel and His Motorcycle Daredevils to host subsequent events.

The timeline below shows Knievel's stunts between June 19, 1966 and September 15, 1968.

June 19, 1966	-----Breaks arm & several ribs trying to jump 12 cars & a van
October 30, 1966 – July 9, 1967	----Successfully jumps between 10 – 16 cars
July 28, 1967	---Serious head injury trying to jump 16 cars
August 18, 1967	--------------Successfully jumps 16 cars
September 24, 1967	---Breaks lower spine trying to jump 16 cars
November 23, 1967 – December 4, 1967	----Successfully jumps 4 motorcycles, 2 vans; 10 cars
December 31, 1967	--Crushes pelvis & femur; fractures hip, wrist, both ankles; concussion, trying to jump Caesar's Palace Fountain in Vegas
May 25, 1968	-Breaks right leg and foot trying to jump 13 cars
July 6, 1968 – September 15, 1968	-Successfully jumps between 8 – 13 cars

PRACTICE TEST ONE

Once A Daredevil, Always A Daredevil

Knievel retired from major performances in January of 1977. At that time, Knievel was rehearsing a jump during which he would jump over a tank full of live sharks. However, during this rehearsal, Knievel lost control of his motorcycle and crashed into a camera man, suffering broken arms.

Robert Craig Knievel passed away on November 30, 2009 after brave battles against diabetes and idiopathic pulmonary fibrosis. Knievel was 69 years old. However, the daredevil spirit of Evel Knievel still lives on today.

29. What structure does the author use to present ideas? (eg: stating a problem and solution, chronological order, cause and effect, compare/contrast) Use **two** details from the passage to support your answer.

_____
_____
_____
_____
_____
_____
_____

30. What additional information does the timeline provide to the reader? Use **two** details from the timeline to support the answer in Part A.

_____
_____
_____
_____
_____
_____

31. You have read two passages about two different daredevils who performed some of the riskiest and dangerous stunts ever recorded in history. However, these two men also experienced their fair share of negative consequences as a result of their daring and fearless personalities.

Your teacher has asked you to write an informational article about the pros and cons of being a daredevil. Be sure to use specific examples, facts and details from **both** passages in your article.

The two texts are:
- "A Tall Order"
- "An Evil Daredevil"

State ELA ASSESSMENT
Grade 4

PRACTICE TEST ONE
Answer Key & Explanations

Practice Test One
Session One
Answer Explanations

1. **A.** Peter can be described as a leader because the island is coming to life and the boys are preparing to greet their captain.
Standard: RL.4.3

2. **D.** D is the best evidence for this. The other answers choices refer either to one of the lost boys, or elements of the story that are not related to Peter's leadership.
Standard: RL.4.3

3. **A.** A main theme of the passage is how a leader can influence their followers. In this case, we know Peter is respected by his follows because the island is coming to life and the lost boys are preparing for his arrival.
Standard: RL.4.1

4. **A.** The quote in answer choice A is the best evidence, as it indicates the island comes to life only when Peter returns. Answer Choice C refers to how the boys and creatures go back to their normal routines when Peter is away. This is not directly as a result of Peter's influence on them. This may have been how they acted before he came to the island.
Standard: RL.4.2

5. **C.** Laziness is a synonym for lethargy.
Standard: RL.4.4

6. **B.** This is prose because it is a narrative text.
Standard: RL.4.6

7. **C.** Passage 1 has more information about how the sun was created. All of the information under the heading, *How did the sun form?* supports this topic.
Standard: RI.4.9, RI.4.1

8. **D.** This is the best evidence from Passage 1 about how the sun was formed as it describes part of the process of the sun formation.
Standard: RI.4.9, RI.4.1

9. **B.** Heat and light are emitted from the sun during nuclear fusion.
Standard: RI.4.1, RI.4.5

10. **B.** Some stars are even bigger than the sun. These stars are called **supergiants**.
Standard: RI.4.4, RI.4.1

11. **D.** The sun has 2 regions, an inner region and an outer region. Each of these regions has 3 additional layers. The sun has much more than 2 layers.
Standard: RI4.1, RI.4.9

12. **B.** Heat and light are *released* from the sun. We know this because they are then *transferred* to Earth.
Standard: RI.4.4

13. **C.** The passage states that 'breaking in' means to teach a horse to wear a saddle and bridle, and to carry on his back a man, woman or child; to go just the way they wish, and to go quietly.."
Standard: RL.4.1

14. **A.** Black Beauty feels that breaking in, or teaching a horse to be ready for a rider and act as her master desires, is necessary.
Standard: RL.4.1

15. **A.** *Start* means to *startle*.
Standard: RL.4.3

16. **B.** The context clue is the phrase "and to go quietly."
Standard: RL.4.4

17. **A.** Black Beauty appreciates the master's gentleness. Black Beauty appreciates that the master gently allows her to become used to the bit slowly, as she mentions in the passage "and so, what with the nice oats, and what with my master's pats, kind words, and gentle ways, I got to wear my bit and bridle." There is no clear evidence for any of the other choices.
Standard: RL.4.3

18. **D.** Various evidence in the text shows that Black Beauty does what she is supposed to do, including that she accepts getting 'broken' in; she wears the bit and bridle and the saddle; she lets the master ride her – all without too much fuss. The other answer choices have no evidence in the text. The master is careful with Black Beauty, but there is not much text evidence for Black Beauty being careful.
Standard: RL.4.1

19. **B.** - this quote from the passage shows clearly that Black Beauty did what she was asked with just a little gentle coaxing – wear a bit and bridle.

- the clue words *my mother always wore one* and *all horses did when they were grown up*, also indicate that Black Beauty is aware of what she is supposed to do.
Standard: RL.4.3

20. **D.** The Navajo grew corn and squash, hunted and ate goats. Buffalo did not live in the desert.

Standard: RI.4.1

21. **A.** The main idea of this paragraph is that the Navajo are desert dwellers and have lived there for a long time, despite changes to the reservation size. The paragraph does not discuss whether it is easy or hard to live in the desert, nor does it mention that the Navaho are the only inhabitants of the desert.

Standard: RI.4.2

22. **C.** The quote "... the Navajo Indian Reservation continues to be located in the southwestern deserts of the United States" provides the best support for Answer Choice "A" in question 21.

Standard: RI.4.1

23. **C.** The mud walls kept the hogan cool in the summer and retained heat in the winter.

Standard: RI.4.1

24. **B.** The paragraph is structured in sequential order as it is describing the weaving process. The word clues are "first", "next," and "last".

Standard: RI.4.5

25. **See detailed explanation.** Student responses will vary. Responses should indicate that Beth and Jo had a very strong, special relationship. Some of the details that support this are:

- Jo didn't leave Beth's side for longer than an hour since Beth told Jo she feels stronger when Jo is by her side.

- Jo feels that being by Beth's side is the greatest honor of her life.

- Jo feels jealous when other nurses care for Beth.

- Jo feels that the hours with Beth are "precious and helpful."

- Jo is grateful for all of the lessons that Beth has taught her.

Standard: RL.4.1, RL.4.3

26. **See detailed explanation.** The theme of this particular section of text is that Beth is slowly preparing herself for her death. In this section, we learn that she is beginning to transition from her life and is beginning to accept that death is upon her. The details that students use will vary, but some examples of the details that support this are:

- "...fit herself for the life to come, by sacred words of comfort, quiet prayers, and the music she loved so well."

- "With the wreck of her frail body, Beth's soul grew strong, and though she said little, those about her felt that she was ready, saw that the first pilgrim called was likewise the fittest, and waited with her on the shore..."

- "...and then, the natural rebellion over, the old peace returned more beautiful than ever..."

Standard: RL.4.1, RL.4.2

27. **See detailed explanation.** To "leave no stone unturned" means to carefully and completely prepare. Some details from the passage that support this meaning are:

- he collected articles, conducted research, and visited the Twin Towers

- he observed the clothing of the construction workers and carried the identification of an American worker so that he and the members of his team could disguise themselves in order to gain access to the twin towers

- they snuck into the towers several times to study everything from the roofs and building layout to information regarding security measures

- Petit carefully planned, prepared, and practiced for what would become one of the most dangerous and risk-taking stunts he would ever perform

Standard: RI.4.4, RI.4.3

28. **See detailed explanation.** Key details that students should include in a summary are:

When Philippe Petit read an article about the construction of the Twin Towers, he immediately began planning and preparing to walk on a wire between them. He practiced and planned for six years. He successfully walked on a wire between the Twin Towers, but was ultimately arrested.

Standard: RI.4.2

29. **See detailed explanation.** The overall structure of the passage is chronological order. Key details that support this are:

- The passage begins with Knievel's birth (Early Life) and ends with his death (Once A Daredevil, Always A Daredevil)

- the events of the story are written in chronological order (Knievel was arrested in 1956, debuted live performances in January 1966)

- timeline shows sequence of events from June 19, 1966 to September 15, 1968

Standard: RI.4.5, RI.4.1

30. **See detailed explanation.** Answers may vary. Suggested student answer: The timeline shows that despite several injuries, Knievel continued to perform. For example, Knievel broke his lower spine trying to jump 16 cars on 9/24/67, but was performing again by 11/23/67. Also, Knievel broke his right leg and foot trying to jump 13 cars on 5/25/68, but was performing again by 7/6/68.

Standard: RI.4.5, RI.4.7

31. **See detailed explanation.** Use the table below for possible examples and facts that students can include in their article.

Pros	Cons
Become famous - Petit's tightrope walk between the Twin Towers is one of the most famous and dangerous tightrope walks *Builds Character* - Petit had to practice and fail many times before he was ready to walk between the Twin Towers - despite numerous injuries, Knievel continued performing motorcycle stunts *Make Money* - the reason Knievel first started performing in the first place was to raise money for his struggling family *Fame Lives On* - Petit goes down in history as the man who walked between the towers - Knievel goes down in history as one of the greatest motorcycle stuntmen to ever live	*Hard work* - Petit practiced and trained for his tightrope walk between the Twin Towers for 6 years *Can Get Seriously Injured* - Knievel suffered injuries such as broken bones and concussions - stunts have life-threatening consequences if failed *Can Get In Trouble* - Petit was arrested after his tightrope walk between the Twin Towers - Knievel was fired from his job after trying to do motorcycle tricks with a bulldozer

Standard: RI.4.9, RI.4.1, RI.4.3

State ELA ASSESSMENT
Grade 4

PRACTICE TEST TWO
Session 1
(Reading)

Directions: Read the poem, then answer the questions below.

Excerpt from The Walrus and the Carpenter
by Lewis Carroll

The Walrus and the Carpenter
Were walking close at hand;
They wept like anything to see
Such quantities of sand:
"If this were only cleared away,"
They said, "it would be grand!"

"If seven maids with seven mops
Swept it for half a year.
Do you suppose," the Walrus said,
"That they could get it clear?"
"I doubt it," said the Carpenter,
And shed a bitter tear.

"O Oysters, come and walk with us!"
The Walrus did beseech.
"A pleasant walk, a pleasant talk,
Along the briny beach:
We cannot do with more than four,
To give a hand to each."

The eldest Oyster looked at him,
But never a word he said:
The eldest Oyster winked his eye,
And shook his heavy head —
Meaning to say he did not choose
To leave the oyster-bed.

But four young Oysters hurried up,
All eager for the treat:
Their coats were brushed, their faces washed,
Their shoes were clean and neat —
And this was odd, because, you know,
They hadn't any feet.

Four other Oysters followed them,

And yet another four;
And thick and fast they came at last,
And more, and more, and more —
All hopping through the frothy waves,
And scrambling to the shore.

The Walrus and the Carpenter
Walked on a mile or so,
And then they rested on a rock
Conveniently low:
And all the little Oysters stood
And waited in a row.

"The time has come," the Walrus said,
"To talk of many things:
Of shoes — and ships — and sealing-wax —
Of cabbages — and kings —
And why the sea is boiling hot —
And whether pigs have wings."

"But wait a bit," the Oysters cried,
"Before we have our chat;
For some of us are out of breath,
And all of us are fat!"
"No hurry!" said the Carpenter.
They thanked him much for that.

"A loaf of bread," the Walrus said,
"Is what we chiefly need:
Pepper and vinegar besides
Are very good indeed —
Now if you're ready, Oysters dear,
We can begin to feed."

"But not on us!" the Oysters cried,
Turning a little blue.
"After such kindness, that would be
A dismal thing to do!"
"The night is fine," the Walrus said.
"Do you admire the view?

"It was so kind of you to come!
And you are very nice!"
The Carpenter said nothing but
"Cut us another slice:
I wish you were not quite so deaf —
I've had to ask you twice!"

"It seems a shame," the Walrus said,
"To play them such a trick,
After we've brought them out so far,
And made them trot so quick!"
The Carpenter said nothing but
"The butter's spread too thick!"

"I weep for you," the Walrus said:
"I deeply sympathize."
With sobs and tears he sorted out
Those of the largest size,
Holding his pocket-handkerchief
Before his streaming eyes.

"O Oysters," said the Carpenter,
"You've had a pleasant run!
Shall we be trotting home again?'
But answer came there none —
And this was scarcely odd, because
They'd eaten every one.

1. How do the Walrus's and the Carpenter's actions reveal differences in their point of view?
    A. The Walrus thinks they should not eat the oysters, while the Carpenter disagrees.
    B. The Carpenter tricks the oysters, while the Walrus tries to warn them.
    C. The Walrus regrets eating the oysters, while the Carpenter doesn't.
    D. Both the Walrus and the Carpenter think twice about eating the oysters, but only the Carpenter eats them in the end.

2. How do the old and young oysters respond to the Walrus differently?
    A. The young and old oysters are both wary of the Walrus.
    B. They old oyster tells the young oysters he is too old to join the Walrus.
    C. The old oyster refuses to join the Walrus, but the young oysters scurry to join.
    D. All of the oysters are confused by the Walrus's request to join him.

3. A theme of the poem can be stated as:
   A. People are cruel while animals are sympathetic.
   B. Young people (or creatures) shouldn't trust those they don't know.
   C. Respect your elders, because they are wise.
   D. It is wrong to take advantage of someone's trust.

4. The poem is a ballad, and uses which form for organization?
   A. prose
   B. rhyming stanzas
   C. setting
   D. characters

5. Read the following line from the 2nd stanza in the poem:
   "I doubt it," said the Carpenter,/ And shed a bitter tear."
   What word or phrase best replaces the word "bitter" in the context of the poem?
   A. sour tasting
   B. excited
   C. rich
   D. unhappy

6. Look at the following image.

   Which two lines from the text does the image portray?
   A. "If seven maids with seven mops/ Swept it for half a year./ Do you suppose...That they could get it clear?"
   B. "The eldest Oyster winked his eye,/ And shook his heavy head"
   C. "Their coats were brushed, their faces washed,/ Their shoes were clean and neat"
   D. "And they rested on a rock/ Conveniently low:/ And all the little Oysters stood/ And waited in a row."

PRACTICE TEST TWO

161

Directions: Read the passage, then answer the questions below.

From: Abe Lincoln Gets His Chance
By Frances Cavanah

Many changes were taking place in the Lincoln cabin. Sarah persuaded Tom to cut two holes in the walls for windows, and she covered them with greased paper to let in the light. He made a wooden door that could be shut against the cold winter winds. Abe and Dennis gave the walls and low ceiling a coat of whitewash, and Sarah spread her bright rag rugs on the new wooden floor.

"Aunt Sairy," Dennis told her, "you're some punkins. One just naturally has to be somebody when you're around."

Abe smiled up at her shyly. "It is sort of like the magic in that story of Sinbad you gave me."

The other children were asleep. Abe sprawled on the floor, making marks on a wooden shovel with a pointed stick. Tom, seated in one of his wife's chairs, was dozing on one side of the fireplace.

Sarah put down her knitting and looked around the cabin. "The place does look right cozy," she replied. "What is that you're doing, Abe?"

"Working my sums."

Tom opened his eyes. "You know how to figure enough already. Put that shovel up and go to bed."

Abe took a knife and scraped the figures from the wooden shovel. He placed it against one side of the fireplace. "Good night, Mamma," he said.

"Good night, Abe."

Sarah's eyes were troubled. She waited until Dennis had joined Abe in the loft, then turned to her husband. "I've been meaning to tell you, Tom, what a good pa you've been to my young ones."

She saw that he was pleased. "I've tried to be a good mother to Abe and Sally, too," she went on.

"You have been, Sairy. They took to you right off."

"I'm right glad, but there's something else I want to talk to you about, Tom." He was nodding again in his chair, and she paused to make sure that he was listening. "Abe's a smart boy. I told him the next time a school keeps in these parts, I'd ask you to let him and the other children go."

"Humph!" Tom grunted. "There ain't any school for him to go to. Anyway, he wastes enough time as 'tis. He's always got his nose buried in those books you brought."

"That bothers me, too. I saw you cuff him the other day because he was reading."

"I had to, Sairy. I told him to come out and chop some wood, but he up and laughed in my face."

"He wasn't laughing at you, Tom. He was laughing at Sinbad."

"Who in tarnation is Sinbad?"

"A fellow in one of his books. Abe said that Sinbad sailed his flatboat up to a rock, and the rock was magnetized and pulled all the nails out of his boat. Then Sinbad fell into the water."

"That's what I mean," Tom exploded. "Dennis told him that book was most likely lies, but Abe keeps on reading it. Where is all this book learning going to get him? More'n I ever had."

"Maybe the Lord meant for young ones to be smarter than their parents," said Sarah, "or the world might never get any better."

7. This passage is an example of which type of writing?
     A. Poetry
     B. Prose
     C. Informational
     D. Drama

8. In the sentence "That bothers me, too. I saw you cuff him the other day because he was reading." What does the word **cuff** mean?
    A. Hit
    B. Praise
    C. Honor
    D. Respect

9. Which sentence in the passage **best** supports a description of Sarah as wise?
    A. "I've tried to be a good mother to Abe and Sally, too," she went on.
    B. "Aunt Sairy," Dennis told her, "you're some punkins. One just naturally has to be somebody when you're around."
    C. "Maybe the Lord meant for young ones to be smarter than their parents," said Sarah, "or the world might never get any better."
    D. Sarah put down her knitting and looked around the cabin. "The place does look right cozy," she replied.

10. Which of the following things did NOT happen when Sarah moved into the Lincoln household?
    A. Tom cut two holes for windows.
    B. Sarah added a kitchen to the house.
    C. Tom built a wooden door for the house.
    D. Abe and Dennis painted the walls.

11. What are Tom's concerns with the story Sinbad?
    A. Sinbad is full of lies.
    B. Abe is not smart enough for the story.
    C. He fears that Abe will start acting like Sinbad.
    D. He worries that Sarah will get his hopes up about school.

12. Which of the following words **best** describes Tom?
    A. Loving
    B. Optimistic
    C. Trusting
    D. Headstrong

Directions: Read the passage and answer the questions below.

Excerpt from Little Women
by Louisa May Alcott

The big house did prove a Palace Beautiful, though it took some time for all to get in, and Beth found it very hard to pass the lions. Old Mr. Laurence was the biggest one; but after he had called, said something funny or kind to each one of the girls, and talked over old times with their mother, nobody felt much afraid of him, except timid Beth. The other lion was the fact that they were poor and Laurie rich; for this made them shy of accepting favors which they could not return. But, after a while, they found that he considered them the benefactors, and could not do enough to show how grateful he was for Mrs. March's motherly welcome, their cheerful society, and the comfort he took in that humble home of theirs. So they soon forgot their pride, and interchanged kindnesses without stopping to think which was the greater.

All sorts of pleasant things happened about that time; for the new friendship flourished like grass in spring. Every one liked Laurie, and he privately informed his tutor that "the Marches were regularly splendid girls." With the delightful enthusiasm of youth, they took the solitary boy into their midst, and made much of him, and he found something very charming in the innocent companionship of these simple-hearted girls. Never having known mother or sisters, he was quick to feel the influences they brought about him; and their busy, lively ways made him ashamed of the indolent life he led. He was tired of books, and found people so interesting now that Mr. Brooke was obliged to make very unsatisfactory reports; for Laurie was always playing truant, and running over to the Marches'.

"Never mind; let him take a holiday, and make it up afterwards," said the old gentleman. "The good lady next door says he is studying too hard, and needs young society, amusement, and exercise. I suspect she is right, and that I've been coddling the fellow as if I'd been his grandmother. Let him do what he likes, as long as he is happy. He can't get into mischief in that little nunnery over there; and Mrs. March is doing more for him than we can."

What good times they had, to be sure! Such plays and tableaux, such sleigh-rides and skating frolics, such pleasant evenings in the old parlor, and now and then such gay little parties at the great house. Meg could walk in the conservatory whenever she liked, and revel in bouquets; Jo browsed over the new library voraciously, and convulsed the old gentleman with

---

benefactors = persons who give money or other help to a person

indolent = lazy

truant = a student who stays away from school/ studies without excuse or explanation

voraciously = eagerly

PRACTICE TEST TWO 165

her criticisms; Amy copied pictures, and enjoyed beauty to her heart's content; and Laurie played "lord of the manor" in the most delightful style.

13. What does the first paragraph reveal about Beth?
    A. She is a very shy person.
    B. She is a very daring person.
    C. She is a strong-willed person.
    D. She is a very adventurous person.

14. Which of the following sentences best summarizes the second paragraph?
    A. Laurie was sick of doing his studies.
    B. Beth was afraid of entering Laurie's house.
    C. The March girls quickly became close friends with Laurie.
    D. Mrs. March disapproved of their friendship.

15. In the second paragraph, what does the phrase "...for the new friendship flourished like grass in spring" mean?
    A. The March girls and Laurie were hostile to each other.
    B. The friendship was slowly growing over time.
    C. The March girls and Laurie were friendly acquaintances.
    D. The friendship grew quickly.

16. In the third paragraph, Mr. Brooke discusses how he acted towards Laurie before he developed a friendship with the March girls. Which of the following statements **best** describes how he treated Laurie before he met he March girls?
    A. "Never mind; let him take a holiday..."
    B. "Let him do what he likes, as long as he is happy."
    C. "I suspect she is right..."
    D. "...I've been coddling the fellow as if I'd been his grandmother."

17. Based on this passage, what can the reader conclude about the March girls?
    A. They're rude and unfriendly to guests.
    B. They are uninterested in people outside of their own family.
    C. They're friendly and welcoming.
    D. They mostly keep to themselves.

18. In the fourth paragraph, what does the word conservatory mean?
    A. A room that contains books
    B. A museum
    C. A music room
    D. A room that contains flowers and plants

Directions: Read the passage and answer the following questions.

The Cottonwool Doctor
by Jean de Wet, Michelle Matthews, and Bridgitte Chemaly Potton

Once upon a time, about 200 years ago, there was a girl called Margaret Ann Bulkly. Margaret lived in a cool, green land called Ireland, in a country called Great Britain.

Margaret was clever and curious. Margaret had big dreams. Margaret was brave and fought when she thought something was wrong.

Margaret's mother and father paid for her brother to be educated as a lawyer. And then they used the last of their money so that he could marry a wealthy man's daughter.

Margaret was clever and had big dreams. But there was no money left for her to study, not even as a governess or a nurse.

Margaret was brave. "I want to be a doctor!" she said. But two hundred years ago a girl could not become a lawyer or a politician or a doctor.

Margaret had an uncle who was a famous painter. His name was James Barry.

One of James Barry's friends was General Miranda from Venezuela. General Miranda had a library – it was very beautiful and very big. His library had more than 6000 books!

"I want to read this one! And this one! And this one!" said Margaret. Margaret was clever and curious. General Miranda was impressed.

When Margaret's uncle James Barry died, he left her some money. "It's enough money to study to be a doctor!" said General Miranda.

"But I can't become a doctor," said Margaret.

"A boy can become a doctor," said General Miranda. "And you can dress like a boy."

Margaret was brave and she pushed for what she believed in. She really wanted to be a doctor. So she cut off her hair. She practiced speaking in a deep voice. She put on boy's clothes.

From then onwards, no one knew that Margaret was a girl. She became James Barry, just like her uncle.

James Barry was a hard-working medical student. He took 13 subjects and worked all through the summer when the other students went on holiday.

But after five years, he nearly didn't get to write his final exam. The examiners thought he looked too young! James Barry didn't have a beard because he wasn't a man.

Dr. James Barry was brave and curious. Dr. James Barry had big dreams. So he joined the army. In the army you would see the world!

In 1816, the army sent Dr. James Barry to Cape Town. Cape Town was a small, interesting city in South Africa. South Africa was far, far away from Ireland.

Dr. James Barry felt excited.

Dr. James Barry was short and slim. He wore platform shoes to look taller and padding under his clothes to look bigger. The people of Cape Town called Dr. James Barry the kapok dokter, the cottonwool doctor.

"I would very much like to cut off your ears!" Dr. James Barry would shout at anyone who challenged him.

Dr. James Barry even once fought a duel with pistols! Luckily, they both missed hitting each other.

Why did the doctor fight so much? Margaret was brave, but she was also frightened. She knew that if anyone found out that she was Dr. James Barry she would no longer be allowed to be a doctor. Everyone had to believe Dr. James Barry was a man.

Dr. James Barry fought when he thought something was wrong.

In Cape Town, people with leprosy were banished to Robben Island. The lepers were put on the island because people believed they could catch the disease from them very easily.

Dirty houses and bad food made the lepers much sicker. Dr. James Barry asked the leaders in Cape Town for cleaner living conditions and healthier food for the sick people on Robben Island.

Many years later Dr. James Barry worked in a war hospital. Here he met Florence Nightingale, a nurse.

Florence Nightingale was also known as The Lady with the Lamp, because she would check on wounded soldiers at night. She became famous during the war because she asked the army leaders for cleaner living conditions and healthier food for the soldiers. Dr. James Barry had been asking for the same things for many years.

Dr. James Barry travelled all over the world. He worked in South Africa, St Helena, Barbados, Mauritius, Trinidad and Tobago, Malta, Corfu, Jamaica, Crimea, West Indies, Canada... 11 places in all.

What exciting adventures he had!

People only found out that Dr. James Barry was a woman when she died in 1865.

In the same year, Dr. Elizabeth Garret Andersen became the first woman to become a doctor in Great Britain.

19. Which of the following statements **best** represents the theme of the passage?
    A. Women can be excellent doctors.
    B. Only men were good doctors.
    C. During the war, the nurses had as much power as the doctors.
    D. Dr. Barry had to go to extreme measures to have the same rights as a man.

20. Which of the following pieces of evidence **best** supports your answer from question 19?
    A. "Dr. James Barry had big dreams. So he joined the army. In the army you would see the world!"
    B. "She knew that if anyone found out that she was Dr. James Barry she would no longer be allowed to be a doctor."
    C. "Many years later Dr. James Barry worked in a war hospital. Here he met Florence Nightingale, a nurse."
    D. "I would very much like to cut off your ears!" Dr. James Barry would shout at anyone who challenged him."

21. What did Dr. Barry do to appear like a man?
    A. Wear platform shoes.
    B. Paint on a fake beard.
    C. Make her head bald.
    D. She spoke in a high voice.

22. Which of the following statements can you infer from the passage?
    A. Florence Nightingale was a very close friend of Dr. Barry
    B. 200 years ago, women and men had equal opportunities.
    C. Dr. Barry was a very timid man.
    D. 200 years ago, women were very limited in what they could do.

23. Which of the following is the **best** evidence to support your answer from Part A?
    A. The only way Margaret could become a doctor is if she pretended to be a man.
    B. Florence Nightingale and Dr. Barry had similar ideas about how to save soldiers.
    C. Dr. Barry wanted to fight everyone.
    D. Dr. Barry enjoyed traveling to South Africa.

24. One can infer from the passage that Margaret/Dr. James Barry was brave. Which pieces of text evidence **best** supports this character trait,
    A. "He took 13 subjects and worked all through the summer when the other students went on holiday.
    B. "She pushed for what she believed in. She really wanted to be a doctor. So she cut off her hair. She practiced speaking in a deep voice. She put on boy's clothes."
    C. "Dirty houses and bad food made the lepers much worse."
    D. "The people of Cape Town called Dr. James Barry the kapok dokter, the cottonwool doctor."

State ELA ASSESSMENT
Grade 4

PRACTICE TEST TWO
Session 2
(Writing)

Directions: Read the following passage and answer the questions.

Excerpt from The Secret Garden
by Frances Hodgson Burnett

Dr. Craven had been waiting some time at the house when they returned to it. He had indeed begun to wonder if it might not be wise to send someone out to explore the garden paths. When Colin was brought back to his room the poor man looked him over seriously.

"You should not have stayed so long," he said. "You must not overexert yourself."

"I am not tired at all," said Colin. "It has made me well. Tomorrow I am going out in the morning as well as in the afternoon."

"I am not sure that I can allow it," answered Dr. Craven. "I am afraid it would not be wise."

"It would not be wise to try to stop me," said Colin quite seriously. "I am going."

Even Mary had found out that one of Colin's chief peculiarities was that he did not know in the least what a rude little brute he was with his way of ordering people about. He had lived on a sort of desert island all his life and as he had been the king of it he had made his own manners and had had no one to compare himself with. Mary had indeed been rather like him herself and since she had been at Misselthwaite had gradually discovered that her own manners had not been of the kind which is usual or popular. Having made this discovery she naturally thought it of enough interest to communicate to Colin. So she sat and looked at him curiously for a few minutes after Dr. Craven had gone. She wanted to make him ask her why she was doing it and of course he did.

"What are you looking at me for?" he said.

"I'm thinking that I am rather sorry for Dr. Craven."

"So am I," said Colin calmly, but not without an air of some satisfaction. "He won't get Misselthwaite at all now I'm not going to die."

"I'm sorry for him because of that, of course," said Mary, "but I was thinking just then that it must have been very horrid to have had to be polite for ten years to a boy who was always rude. I would never have done it."

"Am I rude?" Colin inquired undisturbedly.

"If you had been his own boy and he had been a slapping sort of man," said Mary, "he would have slapped you."

"But he daren't," said Colin.

"No, he daren't," answered Mistress Mary, thinking the thing out quite without prejudice. "Nobody ever dared to do anything you didn't like–because you were going to die and things like that. You were such a poor thing."

"But," announced Colin stubbornly, "I am not going to be a poor thing. I won't let people think I'm one. I stood on my feet this afternoon."

"It is always having your own way that has made you so queer," Mary went on, thinking aloud.

Colin turned his head, frowning. "Am I queer?" he demanded.

"Yes," answered Mary, "very. But you needn't be cross," she added impartially, "because so am I queer–and so is Ben Weatherstaff. But I am not as queer as I was before I began to like people and before I found the garden."

"I don't want to be queer," said Colin. "I am not going to be," and he frowned again with determination.

He was a very proud boy. He lay thinking for a while and then Mary saw his beautiful smile begin and gradually change his whole face.

"I shall stop being queer," he said, "if I go every day to the garden. There is Magic in there–good Magic, you know, Mary. I am sure there is." "So am I," said Mary.

"Even if it isn't real Magic," Colin said, "we can pretend it is. Something is there–something!"

"It's Magic," said Mary, "but not black. It's as white as snow."

25. Choose one of the characters from the passage you have just read. What is one of this character's main character traits? Use **two** pieces of evidence from the text to explain why you chose this character trait.

26. What do Colin and Mary mean when they say the garden has Magic, and what does Mary mean when she says the magic is *white as snow*? Use evidence from the passage to support your response.

Directions: Read the following passage and answer the questions below.

Adapted Excerpt from The Unsinkable Myth
by Richard Howells

There can be no one, surely, reading this article who has not already heard of the Titanic.

And there can be no one among them, equally certainly, who does not already know how the story of the Titanic ends.

This is, when we think about it, really quite remarkable. There is no one alive today who actually was on the Titanic: all the survivors are dead. For the rest of us, there is very little possibility that the disaster has directly affected us, personally or historically.

And yet... as we mark the 100th anniversary of the sinking on April 15th 1912, the world is full of it. We hear the repeated saying: "remember the Titanic" even though not one of us literally can. And yet... ask people and they will tell you not just about the iceberg, but probably also the stories about the lifeboats that took "women and children first", and the band that continued to play "Nearer, My God, to Thee" as the ship sank with the loss of some 1,500 lives. The captain, of course, went down with his ship.

But most of all they will tell you the story of the "unsinkable ship", the biggest and finest ever built, the last word in luxury, that sank on its first and only voyage after crashing into an iceburg. They will say that it was well known that "God himself could not sink this ship", but unfortunately on "her" maiden voyage "she" was duly ripped asunder.

There are two remarkable things about this. First that a 100 year old story continues to be told and re-told. Second that many of the component stories are simply not true. And foremost amongst these is the big one: that prior to its departure from Southampton, the Titanic was celebrated by all as the "unsinkable ship". It wasn't.

So how do we explain all this? The answer is that 100 years on, the sinking of the Titanic has long-since passed from history and into myth.

27. What do you think is a main theme of the passage? Choose **two** pieces of evidence that supports this theme.

_____

_____

28. What makes the story of the Titanic mythical? Use at least **two** details from the passage to support your response.

Directions: Read the passage, then answer the questions below.

The Titanic: A Tragic Adventure

The Making of the Titanic

You have probably heard of the Titanic and its tragic sinking in the Atlantic Ocean. You may have even heard that the ship was one of the biggest ships built at the time. But do you know how it was built and what he inside of the boat actually looked like?

The ship was built to attract wealthy passengers, although it traveled with large numbers of poorer passengers as well, called the third-class passengers. How was the experience of traveling on the Titanic for these two groups of people?

The Price of Fame

The Titanic cost about 7.5 million dollars to build. But this was no ordinary ship. All that money went to building a library, multiple restaurants for the passengers, amenities like a swimming pool and a gym. The ship even included a barber shop! All of this was on top of the fabulous rooms that were built to house the passengers on their voyage.

The rooms on the Titanic were quite luxurious. They included gilded details, paintings in the bedrooms, and artistic carvings to detail the rooms. All of this luxury was meant to tempt the richest passengers to booking their trip on the Titanic, contributing to the ship's reputation as a lavish experience.

The Passengers of the Titanic

The work and money that was put into the Titanic meant that it drew some of the wealthiest and most famous passengers. Onboard was John Jacob Astor IV, who came from a wealthy family and built hotels in New York. Benjamin Guggenheim, who came from a prominent family who made money from mining, was also on the ship. These people were the first-class passengers, whose tickets could cost up to 870 pounds.

Aside from the rich and famous, the Titanic also held about 700 third class passengers. These people were far from rich or famous. Their ticket aboard the Titanic cost between 3-8 pounds. Their rooms were very different from the beautiful lodging that the first-class passengers experienced. The rooms were simple and held bunkbeds for up to ten people. They also didn't have access to the beautiful libraries and restaurants that the wealthy enjoyed. They were given one simple meal a day.

The Sinking

When the Titanic struck the iceberg and began sinking, the lifeboats began to fill up with people. The third-class passengers did not have nearly as much access to the lifeboats and died at much higher rates.

There are several reasons for this. One is that the lives of the wealthy were valued more, and so they got priority when boarding the lifeboats. There were also gates to prevent the third-class passengers from coming to the upper deck, and people got stuck down below. In addition to these physical barriers, many third-class passengers did not speak English. They were confused in the chaos and did not get vital information that could have saved their lives.

After the Titanic

After the sinking of the Titanic, the world was shocked at how many lives were lost. All told, at least 1,500 people died on their trip. People reevaluated what safety measures were necessary for ocean travel. There were new regulations that made sure ships carried enough lifeboats for all the passengers aboard the vessel. The crew and passengers on ships were also required to practice lifeboat drills.

New laws, like the Radio Act of 1912, aimed to make sure that ships would be able to make distress signals to get help from authorities. This law also required ships to keep in radio contact with other ships close by. This way, other vessels would be aware of anything that happened, and could come to the aid of a ship having a problem.

There was even a convention held in London to address the problem of ice in the ocean. This convention established the International Ice Patrol. These ships patrolled the Atlantic Ocean to keep track of dangerous icebergs. They reported the icebergs, and ships traveling across the ocean would avoid the routes that were threatened by the icebergs.

29. What is a main theme of the passage? Use at least **two** pieces of evidence to support your choice.

30. What were the effects of the Titanic sinking? Use **two** pieces of information from the text to support your answer.

31. You've read both the passages 'The Titanic: A Tragic Adventure' and 'The Unsinkable Myth.'

Write a brief article for your school's newspaper about the sinking of the Titanic, including how the sinking affected the passengers on the ship.

Do you think all the stories about the Titanic are true? Explain why you think this way.

Be sure to use specific examples, facts and details from **both** passages to support the points you make in your article.

State ELA ASSESSMENT
Grade 4

PRACTICE TEST TWO
Answer Key & Explanations

Practice Test Two
Answer Explanations

1. **C.** The Walrus shows remorse for eating the oysters, including because he states, "I weep for you." The Carpenter doesn't show remorse because he says nothing but, "The butter's spread too thick!" **(Standard: RL.4.1, RL.4.6)**

2. **C.** The old oyster refuses to join the Walrus, but the young oysters scurry to join. **(Standard: RL.4.1)**

3. **B.** Young people shouldn't trust people they don't know. This is proven in the story because the oysters trust the Walrus and the Carpenter, but they are eventually eaten. **(Standard: RL.4.3)**

4. **B.** The poem is written in rhyming stanzas. **(Standard: RL.4.2)**

5. **D.** The word *bitter* can be replaced with the word *unhappy*. We know the Carpenter is unhappy because the beach is too sandy. **(Standard: RL.5)**

6. **D.** The image shows the Walrus and the Carpenter resting on a rock while all of the oysters are standing in front of them, listening attentively. **(Standard: RL.4.6)**

7. **B.** The passage is prose because it is a narrative text, rather than using a poetic system, dramatic play, or about factual information. **(Standard: RL.4.7)**

8. **A.** Tom believes that Abe is disrespecting him and ignoring his orders, so he hits him or 'cuffs' him to put Abe in his place. **(Standard: RL.4.4)**

9. **C.** Sarah is wise because she understands that Abe is very intelligent, and even though Tom is threatened by education, she knows Abe would thrive if given the opportunity. **(Standard: RL.4.3)**

10. **B.** In the first paragraph, it states that Tom cut holes for windows, added a door, and the two boys (Abe and Dennis) whitewashed the walls. **(Standard: RL.4.1)**

11. **A.** "That's what I mean," Tom exploded. "Dennis told him that book was most likely lies, but Abe keeps on reading it. Where is all this book learning going to get him? More'n I ever had." **(Standard: RL.4.1)**

12. **D.** Tom is headstrong because he is adamant in his belief that academic pursuits will hinder Abe. Tom is headstrong because he believes that Abe doesn't need to go to school. He tells Abe that he already knows his sums, so he doesn't need to keep working. He also tells Sarah that the books Abe reads are just full of lies. **(Standard: RL.4.3)**

13. **A.** Beth is the only family member that is still afraid of Mr. Laurence, and the text refers to her as 'timid', which is another word for shy. **(Standard: RL.4.1)**

14. **C.** The majority of this paragraph is discussing the developing friendship between Laurie and the March girls. This sentence explicitly states that the friendship is growing. **(Standard: RL.4.1, RL.4.2)**

15. **D.** The friendship grew quickly, just like how grass grows quickly in the springtime. **(Standard: RL.4.4)**

16. **D.** This statement shows that the old gentleman thought he was being too protective of Laurie before the friendship with the March girls began. **(Standard: RL.4.1, RL.4.2)**

17. **C.** The March girls take Laurie into their circle, which shows that they're friendly and welcoming people. **(Standard: RL.4.2, RL.4.3)**

18. **D.** Meg explores the palace, so it's clear the word means a room in the house, and she makes bouquets there, which suggests the room contains flowers. **(Standard: RL.4.4)**

19. **D.** The passage explains that the only way Margaret could become a doctor was to pretend she was a man. This was an extreme measure, as she had to impersonate her uncle. **(Standard: RI.4.1)**

20. **B.** Answer choice B has an excerpt from the text that shows how high-stakes and dangerous this was for her. Answer choice D is an extreme thing that the doctor said s/he would do, but it does not particularly relate to attaining the same rights as a man. Rather, it seems more like a personality trait. **(Standard: RI.4.2)**

21. **A.** Margaret did several things to appear like a man. She cut her hair, spoke in a deep voice, and wore platform shoes to appear taller. **(Standard: RI.4.1)**

22. **D.** When Margaret wanted to become a doctor, the only way she could do that was to pretend to be a man. We can infer that women were limited in their possibilities since Margaret had to go to extreme measures to do the same thing a man could do much easier. **(Standard: RI.4.1, RI.4.2)**

23. **A.** Answer Choice A is the only evidence that directly supports the answer in question 22. The other answer choices are either untrue or not relevant to the inference that historically, women were more limited in job choice. **(Standard: RI.4.2, RI.4.8)**

24. **B.** The best evidence for the character trait of "brave" is in answer choice B, as this excerpt shows Margaret always stood up for what she believed in - even when it required a great deal of courage. Answer choice A is incorrect as it would more likely support a trait of 'industrious' or 'hard working'. **(Standard: RI.4.1, RI.4.2)**

25. **Answers will vary.** Example response: One of Mary's main character traits is honesty. For example, when her friend, Colin, asks her "Am I queer?", Mary responds to this hard question with an honest answer and tells him he can sometimes be queer. She also tells Colin clearly and without hesitating that he has been rude to another character, Dr. Craven. For example, when she tells Colin the following: "….but I was thinking just then that it must have been very horrid to have had to be polite for ten years to a boy who was always rude.'" **(Standard: RL.4.1, RL.4.3)**

26. **Answers will vary.** Example Response: Colin and Mary mean that the garden is special, and it is healing for Colin's spirit. When they say the 'Magic' is white as snow, they mean it is good and powerful. Mary believes that the magic in the garden is pure and good, just like white snow. She and Colin believe that the garden is a healing place for him, which is why the magic is good, not dark or scary magic. **(Standard: RL.4.4)**

27. **Answers will vary.** Example Response: One of the main themes of the passage is that the story of the Titanic has changed over time to become myth. The author says that "the sinking of the Titanic has long-since passed from history and into myth." This passage is explaining how the way that we think of the Titanic now is different than how people thought of it at the time. Many stories are told about what happened on the ship that may not be true. For example, the Titanic is known as the 'unsinkable ship', but not everybody thought that 100 years ago. The author is basically saying that as time passes on, the Titanic story has become a myth. **(Standard: RL.4.2, RL.4.3)**

28. **Answers will vary.** Example Response: The story of the Titanic is mythical because it has been passed down through generations, and the details have shifted over time. For example, the myth now claims that the Titanic was called the 'Unsinkable Ship,' but that didn't come about until after the ship sank. Other stories that are told include "women and children first" on the lifeboats, and that the band playing "Nearer, My God, to Thee" as the ship sank. **(Standard: RI.4.2, RI.4.3)**

29. **Answers will vary.** A main theme is that the passengers on the Titanic were treated differently based on their status and how much money they had. The boat had rich first-class passengers, as well as poor third-class passengers whose trip was very different. The rich stayed in fancy bedrooms, and could visit the library, multiple restaurants, and "amenities like a swimming pool and a gym," whereas the shared rooms of third class passengers had only bunk beds. When the Titanic sank, the third class passengers "did not have nearly as much access to the lifeboats and died at much higher rates." For example, first-class passengers were given priority to board the lifeboats, and there were gates to separate the third-class lodging from the rest of the ship, and many poorer passengers could not reach the lifeboats. **(Standard: RI.4.2)**

30. **Answers will vary.** After the sinking of the Titanic, the author states that there were several new rules and regulations that were developed, as the text says in this line: "People reevaluated what safety measures were necessary for ocean travel". New laws, like the Radio Act of 1912, aimed to make sure that ships would be able to make distress signals to get help from authorities. They reported the icebergs, and ships traveling across the ocean would avoid the routes that were threatened by the icebergs. This explains that people began thinking about what needed to be different to ensure a tragedy like this wouldn't happen again. **(Standard: RI.4.21, RI.4.2)**

31. **Answers will vary.** The Titanic is a story that has been told again and again through the years. Because it has been told so many times, it has become a myth. So, we know a lot of about the Titanic, but we might not actually know what was true or not. Before the Titanic was built, it wasn't known as 'The Unsinkable Ship.' It only got that name after it sank! One myth about the Titanic says that only women and children were allowed on the lifeboats, but actually the people who had most access to the lifeboats were the first-class passengers. For example, first-class passengers were given priority to board the lifeboats, and there were gates to separate the third-class lodging from the rest of the ship, and many poorer passengers could not reach the lifeboats. **(Standard: RI.4.1, RI.4.9)**